Cultural Atlas for Young People

ANCIENT EGYPT

Geraldine Harris

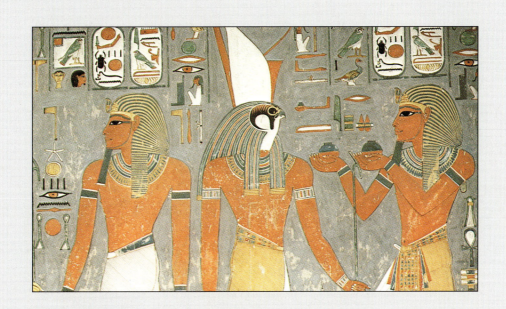

Facts On File

New York • Oxford

Managing Editor: Lionel Bender
Art Editor: Ben White
Designer: Malcolm Smythe
Text Editor: Alison Freegard
Assistant Editor: Madeleine Samuel
Project Editor: Graham Speake
Cartographic Editors: Olive Pearson,
Christine Johnston and Sarah Rhodes
Design Consultant: John Ridgeway
Production: Clive Sparling

Advisory Editor of the series: Gillian Evans,
Fitzwilliam College, Cambridge
Advisory Editor for this volume: John Baines,
Queen's College, Oxford

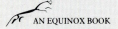
AN EQUINOX BOOK

Planned and produced by:
Equinox (Oxford) Ltd,
Musterlin House,
Jordan Hill Road, Oxford,
England OX2 8DP

Prepared by Lionheart Books

Media conversion and typesetting:
Peter MacDonald, Vanessa Hersey
and Una Macnamara

Copyright © Equinox (Oxford) Ltd 1990

Library of Congress Cataloging-in-Publication
Data

Harris, Geraldine
    Ancient Egypt/Geraldine Harris.
        p. cm. -- (Cultural atlas for young
people).
    Includes index.
    Summary: Maps, charts, illustrations, and
text explore the history and culture of ancient
Egypt.
    ISBN 0-8160-1971-1
    1. Egypt--History--To 640--Juvenile
literature. 2. Egypt--Antiquities--Juvenile
literature. [1. Egypt--History--To 640. 2.
Egypt--Antiquities.] I. Title II. Series
DT83.H33 1989
932--dc19   88-31700
                                            CIP
                                            AC

Published in North America by
Facts On File, Inc.
460 Park Avenue South
New York, N.Y. 10016

Origination by J. Film Process

Third Printing

Printed in Italy

Artwork and Picture Credits
All maps drawn by Lovell Johns, Oxford.

Key: t = top, b = bottom, c = center, l = left, r = right etc
Abbreviations: Ash = Ashmolean Museum, Oxford; BM
British Museum, London; CF = Chris Forsey; EM = Egyptian
Museum, Cairo; GI = Griffith Institute, Ashmolean Museum,
Oxford; KM = Kevin Maddison; ME = Museo Egizio, Turin;
Met = Metropolitan Museum of Art, New York; MH =
Michael Holford, Loughton; RW = Roger Wood, London; WF
= Werner Forman, London.

Title page: Rosalind Hall. 5 John Hillelson Agency. 6-7 M.
Smythe. 8-9 MH. 10 A.A.M van der Heyden. 12t ME. 12b
Hirmer Verlag, Munich. 15, 16 KM. 17l ME (Phaidon Press) .
17tr R. Giveon, Mishmar Ha'emek. 17br University College,
London. 18l Ägyptisches Museum, W. Berlin (Hirmer Verlag,
Munich). 18r Museo Gregoriano Egizio, Vatican (Phaidon
Press). 20t GI (Elsevier). 20b Coral Mula. 21t Rosalind Hall,
London. 21b Coral Mula. 22tl Ash (Elsevier). 22tc Ash (Elsevier). 22tr
Met. 23tl Nina M. Davies, *Ancient Egyptian Paintings*. 23tr
MH. 23b Coral Mula. 24-25 KM. 25 bl MH. 25r Ash (Elsevier).
26c GI (Elsevier). 26bl BM (MH). 26br Ash. (Elsevier). 27 CF.
28l,c Ash. (Elsevier). 28r Ash. (Elsevier). 29 Ash. (Elsevier). 30t EM (RW).
30bl A.A.M van der Heyden, Amsterdam. 30br EM (RWÜ. 31
CF. 32t EM (Hirmer Verlag, Munich). 32bl Brooklyn Museum,
New York. 32br EM (RW). 34t Museo Civico, Bologna (Alinari,
Florence). 34bl D. Johannes, Cairo. 34br EM (RW). 36t A.A.M.
van der Hyden. 36b KM. 38t Coral Mula. 38b, 39 BM. 40-41
KM. 42t EM (RW). 42b Fitzwilliam Museum, Cambridge. 43

Museum of Fine Arts, Boston. 44t University Museum,
University of Pennsylvania. 44bl BM (MH). 44br EM. 46t BM.
46bl A.P. Zivie, Paris. 46bc EM (Drawing: JF). 46br BM. 48l
BM (MH). 48r A.A.M. van der Heyden, Amsterdam. 49t EM
(RW). 49b *The Mastaba of Mereruka*, Chicago. 50-51 Robert
Harding Picture Library. 52-53 D. Barnard, London. 54 GI. 56
RW. 56-57 KM. 57br CF. 58 RW. 60l A.A.M. van der Heyden,
Amsterdam. 60r A.-P. Zivie, Paris. 61l A.A M. van der
Heyden, Amsterdam. 61r Institute of Archaeology, University
of London (RAF). 62 John Hillelson Agency, London. 63
A.A.M. van der Heyden, Amsterdam. 64t Rosalind Hall,
London. 64c MH. 64b, 65t A.A.M. van der Heyden,
Amsterdam. 65b Hirmer Verlag, Munich. 66t WF. 66b MH.
67t A.-P. Zivie, Paris. 67b Rosalind Hall, London. 68 GI. 68-69
KM. 69 John Hillelson Agency, London. 70 A.M. Calverley,
The Temple of King Sethos at Abydos, London & Chicago. 71
A.-P. Zivie, Paris. 72 A.A.M. van der Heyden, Amsterdam. 73l
Ash (Elsevier). 73r J. Baines, Oxford. 74t Met. 74b D.
Johannes, Cairo. 76l Museum of Fine Arts, Boston. 76r
Rosalind Hall, London. 77t A.A.M. van der Heyden,
Amsterdam. 77c D. Barnard, London. 77b Ash (Elsevier). 78,
79 CF. 80t Ash (Elsevier). 80b RW. 82t EM (Drawing: JF). 82bl
Rosalind Hall, London. 82br EM (Hirmer Verlag, Munich). 83l
EM (RW). 83cr Rosalind Hall, London. 83br Egypt Exploration
Society, London. 84t Staatliche Museum, E. Berlin. 84b D.
Johannes, Cairo. 85t J. Baines, Oxford. 85b A.A.M. van der
Heyden. 86-87 CF. 88 Museo Civico, Bologna (Fotofast,
Bologna). 90l Ash (Elsevier). 90r Brooklyn Museum, NY. 91l
EM (RW). 91r Romer-Pelizaeus-Museum, Hildesheim.

CONTENTS

INTRODUCTION

This book is about ancient Egypt, one of the great civilizations of the past. The ancient Greeks saw Egypt as the source of all wisdom. Roman emperors traveled to Egypt to marvel at monuments such as the pyramids. Egyptian statues and obelisks were sent to decorate Rome. The worship of Egyptian gods and goddesses like Isis and Osiris spread through the Roman Empire as far as Britain.

The modern fascination with Egypt began in the late 18th century. Since then a huge number of ancient towns, temples and tombs have been excavated. No country in the world has so many impressive ancient remains as Egypt does. In the Nile Valley the past seems very close. The people who lived there thousands of years ago have left us a wonderful legacy of art and architecture and literature.

Ancient Egypt is divided into two main sections. The first, **The History of the Pharaohs**, tells the story of Egypt from the union of the country in about 2920 BC to the coming of the Romans almost 3,000 years later. Archeologists break up the great span of Egyptian history into a series of periods and "kingdoms." You can see how this works by looking at the Table of Dates on pages 6 and 7.

The Predynastic Period was the era before Egypt was united under a single ruler. From the Early Dynastic Period, Egypt was ruled by dynasties of kings. A dynasty was a sequence of rulers, usually related by blood or marriage. The eras known as kingdoms were times when Egypt was strong and united. The "intermediate periods," which come between or after kingdoms, were times when the country was weak and divided. The last dynasties of native Egyptian kings ruled during the Late Period, so called because it comes at the end of Egypt's history

as an independent nation. In the Greco-Roman Period, Egypt was first under Greek and then under Roman rule.

On each history double-page spread you will find a list of the dynasties that reigned during that period or kingdom. The names and dates of the most important rulers in each dynasty are also given. The exact spelling and pronunciation of most ancient Egyptian names is uncertain because vowels were not written in full. Ideas about how the names should be written out in English have changed as our knowledge of ancient languages has grown. The name that used to be spelled Tutankhamen is now usually written as Tutankhamun or Tutankhamon. It means "Living Image of the god Amon."

The maps in the first part of the book are linked to topics in the text. They show you which places were important in each period or kingdom or sites where objects of a particular date have been found.

The second part of this book, **A Journey Down the Nile,** takes you the length of Egypt. The journey starts in Lower Nubia, a country to the south of Egypt, and ends at the Mediterranean coast. There is a map for each region. These are maps of modern Egypt but they mark all the important ancient sites and structures that survive. For most sites a modern Arabic name and at least one ancient name are given. Some of these ancient names are Egyptian. Others date to the time when the Greeks ruled Egypt. Beside the site names are symbols to show you what kind of ancient remains have been found there.

The Glossary on pages 92-93 explains the Egyptian, Greek and archeological terms used in this book. If you want to look up a particular place, the Gazeteer on pages 94 will tell you how to locate it.

Abbreviations used in this book
AD = Anno Domini (The Year of the Lord: of the Christian era).
BC = before Christ. c. = circa (about). In the King lists, Q = Queen. in = inch. ft = foot. mi = mile.

▷ Detail of a granite statue with added cartouche, from Luxor.

TABLE OF DATES

	4500 BC	3500 BC	3000 BC	2500 BC
EGYPTIAN HISTORY	**Predynastic** Badarian culture, Nile valley 4500-4000. Merimda culture, Delta 4800-4000. Faiyum culture 5500-4200.	**Predynastic** Naqada I, Nile valley 4000-3500. Naqada II, Nile valley 3500-2920. Lower Egypt cultures 3500-3000.	**Foundation of Egyptian state** c.3050. Trade with Mesopotamia. **Early Dynastic Period** 2920-2575. Ist – 3rd Dynasties. First mining expeditions to Sinai.	**Old Kingdom** 2575-2134. 4th – 6th Dynasties. Raids on Libya, Palestine and Lower Nubia. Trade with Upper Nubia. **First Intermediate Period** 2134-2040 7th – 11th Dynasties. Rival dynasties and civil wars.
	Hunters from stone palette, c. 3000 BC.		Tomb stela of King Wadj from Abydos, c. 2850 BC.	Statue of King Khephren from Giza, c. 2495 BC.
ARCHITECTURE AND TOMBS	Reed huts. Graves under hut floors at Merimda Beni Salama.	Reed shrines. First buildings in mudbrick. Walled town and brick-lined tombs at Hierakonpolis.	Mudbrick 'funerary palaces' at Abydos. Mudbrick mastaba tombs at Saqqara. First stone buildings. Step pyramids at Saqqara.	Massive stone pyramids and stone mastaba tombs at Giza, Saqqara and Abusir. Stone sun temples and obelisks at Abu Ghurab and Abusir.
				Painting of geese from a tomb at Maidum, c. 2560 BC.
			Step Pyramid of King Djoser at Saqqara, c. 2560 BC.	
	Painted terracotta figurine of a dancer, c. 4000 BC.			
ART AND CRAFTS	Fine pottery vessels, clay figurines, objects carved from ivory.	Painted pottery, stone palettes and vessels, terracotta and ivory figurines. First wall paintings and stone statuettes.	Large stone statues. First reliefs in wood and stone. First stone stelae. Gold jewelry. Faience figurines.	Painted tomb reliefs of daily life. Royal statues in hard stones or in copper. Private statues in stone or wood. Furniture in wood and decorated sheet gold.

2000 BC	1500 BC	1300 BC	1000 BC	300 BC
Middle Kingdom 2040-1640 11th – 13th Dynasties. Reunion of Egypt under Theban dynasty. Trade with Syria and Palestine. Occupation of Lower Nubia. **Second Intermediate Period** 1640-1532. 14th – 17th Dynasties. Occupation of Delta by Hyksos from Syria/Palestine. Kerma culture occupies Lower Nubia. War between the Hyksos and Theban kings.	**Early New Kingdom** 1550-1307 17th – 18th Dynasties. Egypt reunited under Theban dynasty. Conquest of Lower and Upper Nubia. Rise of Egyptian empire in Syria and Palestine.	**Late New Kingdom** 1307-1196. 19th – 20th Dynasties. Wars against the Hittites in Syria. Depopulation of Lower Nubia. Wars against the Sea Peoples. Gradual loss of Near Eastern empire.	**Third Intermediate Period** 1070-712 21st – 25th Dynasties. Egypt divided. Kings ruling Delta and High Priests ruling Thebes. Rise of Nubian Kingdom of Napata. Civil wars among petty rulers. **Late Period** 712-332. 25th-30th Dynasties Egypt reunited by Nubian kings. Conquest of Egypt by the Assyrians and by the Persians. Periods of native rule between conquests.	**Graeco-Roman Period** 332 BC- AD 395. Greek rule 332-30 BC. Egypt ruled by Ptolemies. Many Greek immigrants. Some Egyptian rebellions. Roman rule 30 BC-AD 395 Egypt becomes part of the Roman Empire. Most of Nubia ruled by Kings of Meroe.

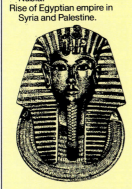

Statue of King Senwosret III from Deir el-Bahri, c. 1850 BC.

Gold mask from the mummy of King Tutankhamon, c. 1325 BC.

Colossal statue at the Great Temple of Abu Simbel, c. 1270 BC.

Kneeling Egyptian from statue base of a Persian king, c. 500 BC.

Head of a priest in green schist, c. 75 BC.

Stone mortuary temple of Mentuhotpe III at Deir el-Bahri. Mudbrick pyramids in Middle Egypt and at Dashur. Rock-cut tombs in Middle Egypt. Forts in Nubia.	Terraced temple of Hatshepsut at Deir el-Bahri. Rock-cut royal tombs in the Valley of the Kings. Temples of Amon at Karnak and Luxor. Palaces and Aten temples at el-Amarna.	Mortuary temples of Ramesses II (The Ramesseum) and Ramesses III (Medinet Habu) at Thebes. Great Hypostyle Hall at Karnak, Ramesses II. Great Temple of Abu Simbel and other rock-cut and freestanding temples in Nubia.	Temple of Amon at Tanis with underground royal tombs. Large tombs with mudbrick pylons at Thebes. Shaft tombs at Saqqara. Granite temple of Isis at Behbeit el-Hagar.	Great Egyptian-style temples at Philae, Kom Ombo, Edfu, Esna and Dendara. Graeco-Egyptian style 'funerary houses' at Tuna el-Gebel. Underground galleries of tombs at Alexandria.

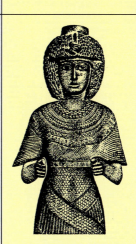

Relief of a blind harpist from a Saqqara tomb c.1300 BC.

Facade of the temple of Hathor at Dendara, c. AD 34

Wooden figurine of a servant from a Theban tomb, c. 2020 BC.

Relief from a vizier's tomb at Thebes, c. 1360 BC.

Inlaid bronze figure of a High Priestess, c. 850 BC.

Royal portrait sculpture. Tomb paintings of daily life. Painted wooden models of daily life. Fine jewelry in gold and semi-precious stones.	Temple reliefs with royal and religious scenes. Monumental sculpture. Tomb paintings and painted reliefs of daily life. Cosmetic containers in wood, ivory or faience. Decorated pottery and faience vessels.	Colossal stone statues. Temple reliefs with battle and hunting scenes. Illustrated 'Books of the Dead'. Tomb paintings of religious scenes.	Faience bowls and chalices. Bronze figurines. Private sculpture in hard stones. Decorated cartonnage coffins and stone sarcophagi.	Portrait sculpture in hard stones. Temple reliefs of religious scenes. Faience and terracotta figurines. Painted 'mummy portraits'.

PART ONE

THE HISTORY OF THE PHARAOHS

△ Detail from the golden throne found in Tutankhamon's tomb by the English Egyptologist Howard Carter in 1922.

▷ The 4,500-year-old pyramids at Giza, to the south-west of Cairo, the present-day capital of Egypt. The two largest are more than 330ft high.

8

EGYPT, GIFT OF THE NILE

About 12,000 years ago most of North Africa was covered by savannah – grasslands with large populations of animals. Gradually the climate became drier and the savannah turned to desert. The river Nile flowed through this desert, with rich vegetation along its valley.

The Nile valley is a long, narrow corridor, never more than 12mi and sometimes only 1mi wide. Before joining the Mediterranean, the river splits into many branches. This Delta area is some 125mi across.

The Black Land and the Red Land

The ancient Egyptians called their country the Black Land. Black was the color of the rich soil in the Nile valley. The valley had once been a swamp, but as the climate changed only the Delta retained large areas of marshland.

Every year summer rains in Africa caused the waters of the Nile to rise along its length, flooding the low-lying fields in Egypt for about two months. The area covered in water was known as the floodplain and the event the inundation. When the waters went down they left a layer of fertile mud ideal for growing crops in. The level of the inundation was important. A low ("bad") Nile meant that only part of the floodplain would be covered and not enough crops could be grown to feed everyone. A very high Nile (also called bad) might flood villages and towns.

To the east and west of the Nile valley lie the deserts, which the Egyptians called the Red Land. The valley-dwellers thought of the Red Land as a dangerous and sinister place. The few oases in the Western Desert were sometimes used as prison camps. The mountainous Eastern Desert was divided by dry river beds called wadis which occasionally filled after heavy rains. These wadis became trade routes across the desert to the coast of the Red Sea.

South of Egypt the Nile becomes difficult to sail because of the rapids known as the Cataracts. To the north, Egypt was protected by the marshes of the Delta. These natural barriers made Egypt a difficult country to invade. Its isolation from the rest of the ancient world helps to explain the unique culture of Egypt.

▽ An ancient scene in modern Egypt at Abusir near Cairo. Palms are growing in the arable land. The pyramids are nearly 4,500 years old.

▷ The geography of Egypt today. The Nile is fed by the Blue and the White Nile. Its ultimate source is Lake Victoria, in the south of Uganda.

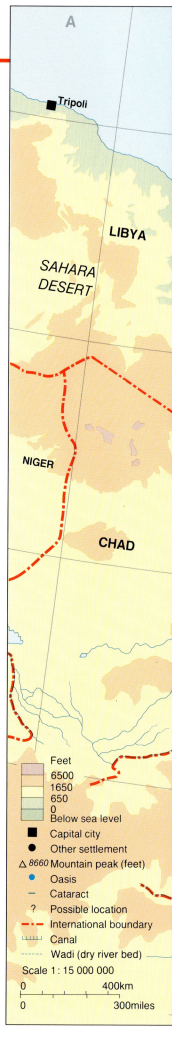

LIBYA

SAHARA DESERT

NIGER

CHAD

Feet
6500
1650
650
0
Below sea level
■ Capital city
● Other settlement
△ 8660 Mountain peak (feet)
● Oasis
– Cataract
? Possible location
–·– International boundary
⊔⊔⊔ Canal
---- Wadi (dry river bed)

Scale 1 : 15 000 000

0   400km
0   300miles

THE LAND OF GOLD

The desert hills on the edge of the Nile provided limestone, sandstone and granite for building temples and tombs. Rarer stones such as diorite, alabaster and basalt were mainly used for vases and statues.

The Egyptian deserts also contained various semiprecious stones and precious metals – particularly gold. One foreign king wrote to Pharaoh that it was well known that in Egypt gold was as common as dust.

The Nile – Egypt's first resource

The most precious resource in ancient Egypt was water. The inundation made it possible to grow cereal crops such as corn and barley. Another major crop was flax. This was spun into linen. The best ancient Egyptian linen is so fine that you can see through it.

Irrigation channels were dug to carry water far from the Nile to gardens and orchards. Vegetables such as lettuce, onions, peas and lentils were raised, and fruits such as pomegranates and figs were grown.

Wet clay from the riverbank was shaped into bricks that were left to dry in the sun. All Egyptian houses were built in this mud brick.

▷ Pieces from the oldest known map, dating to the 12th century BC. The map shows stone quarries and gold mines in the Wadi Hammamat, a valley in the Eastern Desert. It was used by an expedition sent to bring back a colossal royal statue cut in the quarries. The Egyptian script mentions both natural and man-made landmarks.

▽ In this scene from a 19th-Dynasty tomb a couple are working in paradise – which is of course just like Egypt. In the top row they cut heads of corn. The middle row shows them harvesting flax and plowing a field. Below is a garden with date-palms and ornamental plants.

Only in the Delta was there enough grass to feed large numbers of cattle so most herds were kept there. The marshes were very rich in fish, bird and plant life. The Egyptians caught fish with nets or spears and hunted birds with boomerangs. Lotus flowers were gathered to make perfumes and reeds were cut to build boats or to weave into matting. The stems of papyrus plants were made into a kind of paper – one of Egypt's chief exports (see pages 22-23).

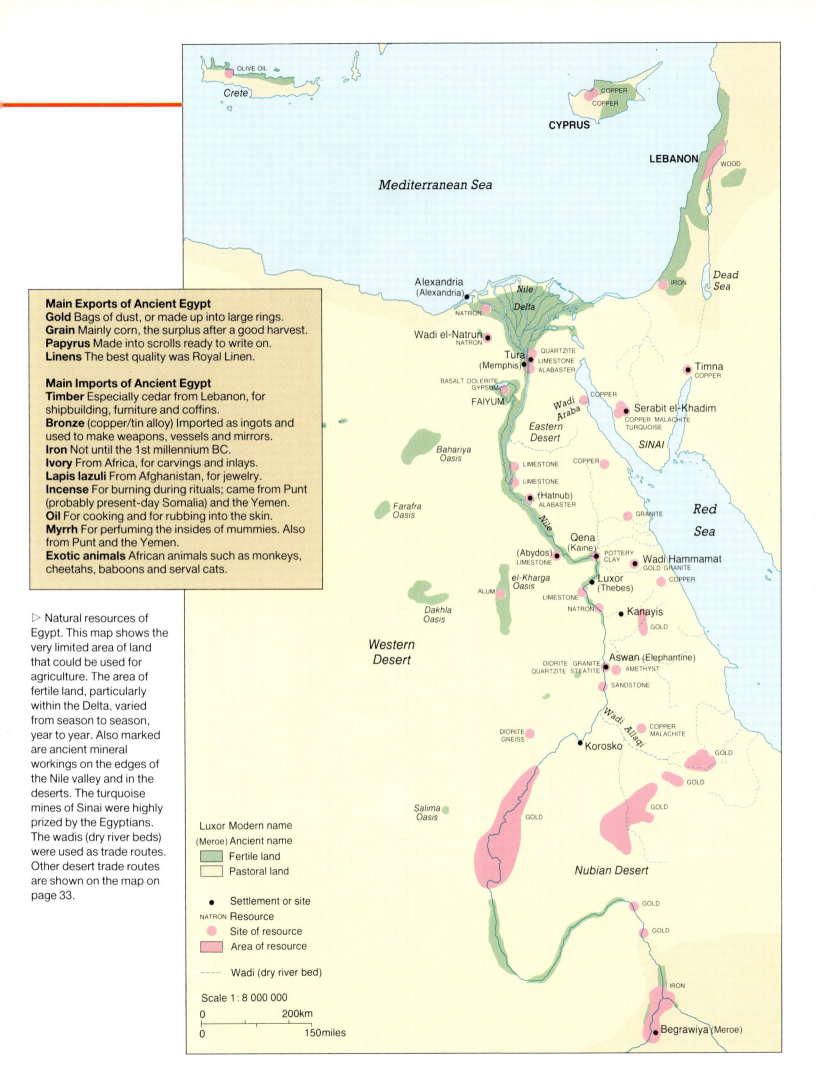

Main Exports of Ancient Egypt
Gold Bags of dust, or made up into large rings.
Grain Mainly corn, the surplus after a good harvest.
Papyrus Made into scrolls ready to write on.
Linens The best quality was Royal Linen.

Main Imports of Ancient Egypt
Timber Especially cedar from Lebanon, for shipbuilding, furniture and coffins.
Bronze (copper/tin alloy) Imported as ingots and used to make weapons, vessels and mirrors.
Iron Not until the 1st millennium BC.
Ivory From Africa, for carvings and inlays.
Lapis lazuli From Afghanistan, for jewelry.
Incense For burning during rituals; came from Punt (probably present-day Somalia) and the Yemen.
Oil For cooking and for rubbing into the skin.
Myrrh For perfuming the insides of mummies. Also from Punt and the Yemen.
Exotic animals African animals such as monkeys, cheetahs, baboons and serval cats.

▷ Natural resources of Egypt. This map shows the very limited area of land that could be used for agriculture. The area of fertile land, particularly within the Delta, varied from season to season, year to year. Also marked are ancient mineral workings on the edges of the Nile valley and in the deserts. The turquoise mines of Sinai were highly prized by the Egyptians. The wadis (dry river beds) were used as trade routes. Other desert trade routes are shown on the map on page 33.

Luxor Modern name
(Meroe) Ancient name
▮ Fertile land
▯ Pastoral land
● Settlement or site
NATRON Resource
⬤ Site of resource
▰ Area of resource
--- Wadi (dry river bed)

Scale 1 : 8 000 000
0 — 200km
0 — 150miles

THE TWO KINGDOMS

The rulers of ancient Egypt were known as the Lords of the Two Lands – the Kings of Upper and Lower Egypt. Upper Egypt was the narrow Nile valley. Lower Egypt was the north, particularly the Delta. The Two Lands were first united under one ruler about 2920 BC. The site of the capital of the union changed as families from different areas came to the throne. Several of these capital cities are located near the boundary of Upper and Lower Egypt, an area sometimes known as Middle Egypt.

Administrative centers

Until Greco-Roman times the population of ancient Egypt was probably never much higher than four million people. Both Upper and Lower Egypt were divided into districts called nomes, each with its administrative center. These centers would not have been large. Most Egyptians lived on farms or in small villages. Each village had a headman and each nome a governor, or nomarch. The nomarchs ruled their districts on behalf of the kings but if the central government was weak they often tried to take power for themselves. Among the nomarchs' most important jobs were the upkeep of dykes and irrigation channels and the storing and distribution of grain to feed the local population during famines.

The first civil servants

In the capital of Egypt a very large number of officials worked for the central government. The most important official was the vizier. He was in charge of justice and public works. At some periods there were two viziers, one for Upper and one for Lower Egypt. The vizier's office oversaw the collection of taxes. Until it came under Greek rule, Egypt had no coinage. All taxes had to be paid with goods such as grain and cattle. A register of land ownership was kept and every two years all the cattle in Egypt were counted.

The officials who worked under the vizier had to be good at many jobs. One official, Weni, tells us in an inscription that during his career he was an inspector of pyramids, a judge and a tax collector. Weni led an army, supervised the digging of canals and the quarrying of stone for pyramids, and eventually became governor of the whole of southern Egypt.

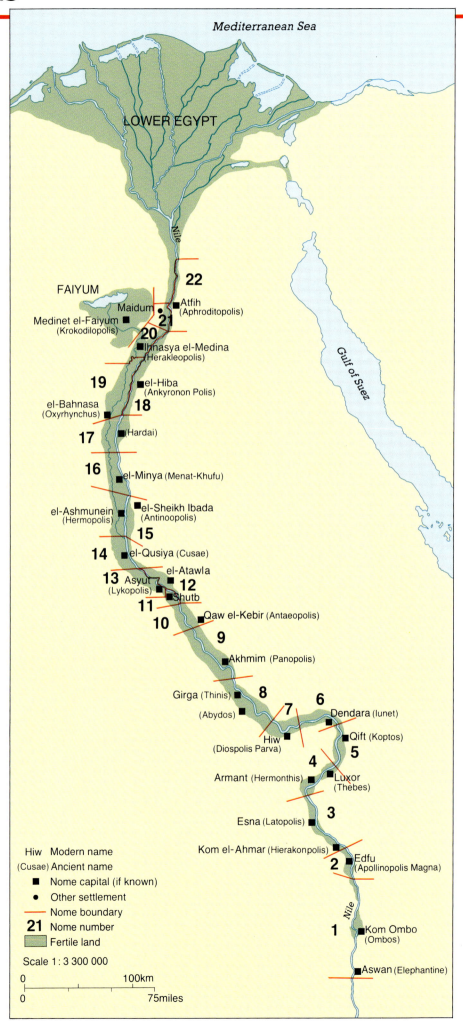

Upper Egypt

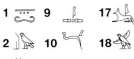

1	9	17
2	10	18
3	11	19
4	12	20
5	13	21
6	14	22
7	15	
8	16	

Lower Egypt

1	8	15
2	9	16
3	10	17
4	11	18
5	12	19
6	13	20
7	14	

▷ A nomarch, seated, oversees the cattle census. Cattle are driven past a kiosk to be counted and recorded by the scribes. The owners were then told how much tax they would have to pay.

△ Each district, or nome, had a symbol. These symbols or ensigns were often derived from the form of a local god or goddess. In temple reliefs (carved scenes) the symbols are worn on the heads of figures who represent the nomes.

◁ The nomes of Upper Egypt. The boundaries of the 22 nomes are based on a Middle Kingdom nome list. Some nomes had more than one capital town during their history. In others the site of the capital is uncertain.

▷ Lower Egypt was divided into 20 nomes. This map is based on nome lists in temples of the Greek and Roman (Greco-Roman) periods. Nome boundaries in the Delta were formed by the branches of the Nile.

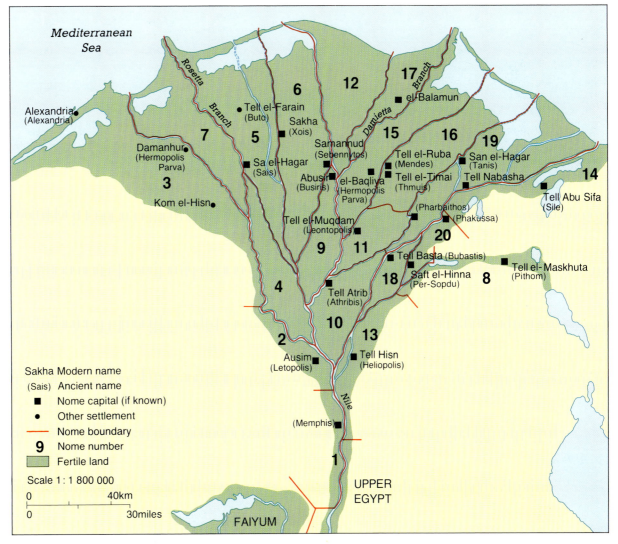

Mediterranean Sea

Alexandria (Alexandria)

Rosetta Branch

Damietta Branch

Nile

12 17 6

Tell el-Farain (Buto)

Sakha (Xois)

el-Balamun

7 5

15 16 19

Damanhur (Hermopolis Parva)

Samannud (Sebennytos)

Tell el-Ruba (Mendes)

San el-Hagar (Tanis)

Sa el-Hagar (Sais)

Tell Nabasha

3

Abusir (Busiris)

el-Baqliya (Hermopolis Parva)

Tell el-Timai (Thmuis)

14

Kom el-Hisn

Tell Abu Sifa (Sile)

Tell el-Muqdam (Leontopolis)

Pharbaithos

Phakussa

20

9 11

Tell Basta (Bubastis)

4

18

Saft el-Hinna (Per-Sopdu)

8

Tell el-Maskhuta (Pithom)

Tell Atrib (Athribis)

10 13

2

Tell Hisn (Heliopolis)

Ausim (Letopolis)

Sakha Modern name
(Sais) Ancient name
■ Nome capital (if known)
● Other settlement
— Nome boundary
9 Nome number
▨ Fertile land

Scale 1 : 1 800 000

0 40km
0 30miles

(Memphis)

1

UPPER EGYPT

FAIYUM

THE POWER OF PHARAOH

From about 1350 BC the king of Egypt was known as Pharaoh. The word means "The Great House" – the royal palace. The king had several palaces. He traveled between them on tours of inspection and was supposed to visit each part of the country at least once every two years.

In theory the king had absolute power but he had to govern Egypt through his officials. Finding officials who would be honest and loyal always seems to have been a problem. Some kings led the army in person against foreign enemies or rebels. The king was also head of the legal system. The Egyptians believed that when the world was made out of chaos the Creator also made *maat*, which means order, truth and justice. The king had to be the champion of *maat* and the enemy of chaos.

Divine kings

Egyptian kings were thought to get their authority from the gods and to be in some ways godlike or divine, themselves. During his lifetime the king was identified with the hawk god Horus who overcame the evil god Set. In his role as high priest, the king was expected to build temples for the gods and to keep them happy with gifts and sacrifices.

Much of the king's time was taken up with elaborate ceremonies that were believed to ensure the well-being of Egypt. The king was held responsible for making the Nile rise to the right level (a "good" Nile) and the crops grow.

One of the most important royal ceremonies was the Sed festival, which was first celebrated in the 30th year of a king's reign. The purpose of this festival, which included a ritual race, was to persuade the gods to renew the king's strength and to grant him a long life.

Royal burials

The king would prepare for death by building himself a splendid tomb and a temple in which his spirit, or *ka*, would be worshiped as a god. In death, the king was identified with the god Osiris. According to Egyptian myth, Osiris was murdered by his brother Set but came back to life to rule over the spirits of the dead. In early times the Egyptians believed that everyone's chance of a life after death depended on the dead king being accepted among the gods.

▽ A king taking part in the daily temple ritual. He opens a gilded shrine and makes offerings to a statue of the god Amon. The chief offering is a figurine of the goddess who represents *maat*. This symbolizes the king's duty to uphold truth, justice and order. On the table are vegetables, fruit and joints of meat offered as a meal for the god. On the circular stand in front of the shrine incense was burned to fill the sanctuary with scented smoke. The priestess, center right, shakes a sacred rattle called a sistrum.

△ A relief of King Sekhemkhet, from copper mines in Sinai, about 2605 BC. The rock inscriptions were discovered in 1973.

◁ In this granite statue King Ramesses II is shown as a handsome young man wearing the Blue or War Crown. He holds a crook to show that he is the shepherd of his people. On the crown is an *uraeus*, an image of the cobra goddess spitting fire at the enemies of Egypt.

▽ King Senwosret I runs the Sed festival race carrying a sacred oar and a *hepet* – perhaps part of a ship's steering gear. He is wearing the Red Crown of Lower Egypt.

RULERS OF EGYPT

The Egyptians believed that a person's life was bound up in his name. You could help the dead by speaking their names aloud or destroy them by erasing their names wherever they appeared. Each Egyptian king had at least five names. The most important were the throne name and the birth name. Throne names such as Menkheperre ("Enduring like the forms of Ra") were taken at a king's coronation. Birth names such as Amonhotep ("Amon is gracious") were family names used from childhood. These two names were usually written inside a cartouche, an oval of rope symbolizing "everything which the Sun encircles." By putting their cartouches on objects, Egyptian kings were claiming to rule the world.

Egyptian history is divided into dynasties,

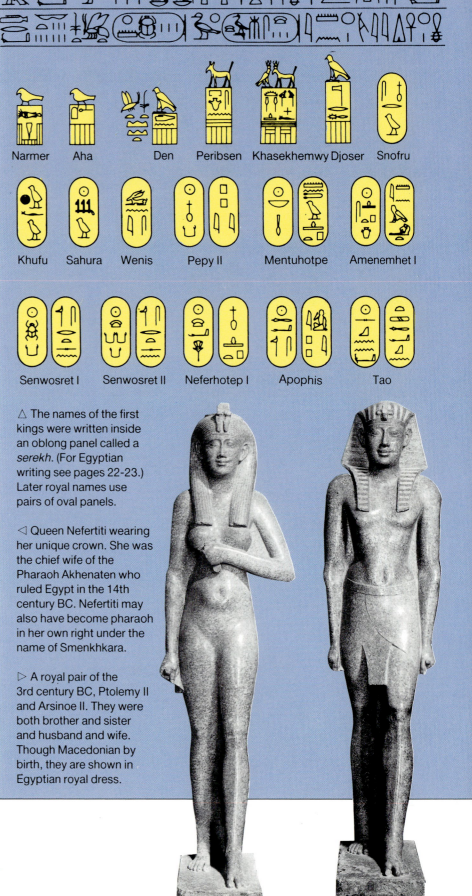

Narmer Aha Den Peribsen Khasekhemwy Djoser Snofru

Khufu Sahura Wenis Pepy II Mentuhotpe Amenemhet I

Senwosret I Senwosret II Neferhotep I Apophis Tao

△ The names of the first kings were written inside an oblong panel called a *serekh*. (For Egyptian writing see pages 22-23.) Later royal names use pairs of oval panels.

◁ Queen Nefertiti wearing her unique crown. She was the chief wife of the Pharaoh Akhenaten who ruled Egypt in the 14th century BC. Nefertiti may also have become pharaoh in her own right under the name of Smenkhkara.

▷ A royal pair of the 3rd century BC, Ptolemy II and Arsinoe II. They were both brother and sister and husband and wife. Though Macedonian by birth, they are shown in Egyptian royal dress.

See also pages 48-49.

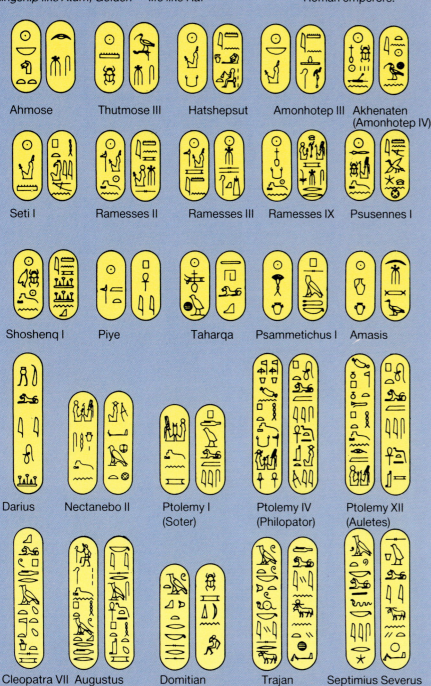

◁ A typical full royal name in hieroglyphics: "Horus, Mighty Bull, full of glorious appearances, [under the protection of] The Two Ladies, enduring of Kingship like Atum, Golden

Horus, Strong of arm, Defeater of the Nine Bows, He of the Sedge and the Bee, Menkheperrure, Son of Ra, Thutmose (IV), beloved of Amon-Ra, given life like Ra."

▽ Royal names became more complicated in the later dynasties and Ptolemaic Period. In the bottom row are Egyptian names and titles of some Roman emperors.

Ahmose Thutmose III Hatshepsut Amonhotep III Akhenaten (Amonhotep IV)

Seti I Ramesses II Ramesses III Ramesses IX Psusennes I

Shoshenq I Piye Taharqa Psammetichus I Amasis

Darius Nectanebo II Ptolemy I (Soter) Ptolemy IV (Philopator) Ptolemy XII (Auletes)

Cleopatra VII (Philopator) Augustus Domitian Trajan Septimius Severus

groups of rulers usually related by birth or marriage. An Egyptian king always had a chief queen known as the Great Royal Wife. He might also have a large number of less important wives who made up the royal harem. The Great Royal Wife was often the king's full or half-sister. The ancient Egyptians had no law against marriage between close relatives, but such marriages only seem to have been common among royalty. See also pages 48-49.

How kings were chosen

The crown prince was usually the eldest son of the king and his chief queen. If the Great Royal Wife had no son an heir had to be chosen from among the children of the lesser wives. There seems to have been no clear rule about how this was to be done. Sometimes the Egyptian gods are said to have made the choice.

One story tells how a prince fell asleep close to the Great Sphinx at Giza. The sphinx god appeared to the prince in a dream and complained that the desert sand had almost covered its body. The Sphinx promised that if the prince got the sand cleared away he would become ruler of Egypt. The prince did as he was asked and later became King Thutmose IV. Sometimes an important person of non-royal birth became ruler of Egypt by marrying the eldest daughter of a king and his chief queen.

The coronation of Pharaoh

It seems to have been the ritual of the coronation, rather than royal blood, that was thought to give a king divine power. He was crowned with the Double Crown – the White Crown of Upper Egypt and the Red Crown of Lower Egypt. His costume included other symbols of his power. He wore a bull's tail attached to his kilt to show that he had the strength of a mighty bull. Egyptian men were usually clean-shaven but the king wore a false beard to imitate the lapis-lazuli beards of the gods.

Royal jewelry often included images of the "Two Ladies," the vulture goddess of the south and the cobra goddess of the north.

Everything about the king was intended to project the image of a god on earth. In practice, a king's status varied from period to period. Some rulers were more successful at claiming divinity than others.

THE GODS OF EGYPT

The Egyptians told many stories about the creation of the world. Most of them start by imagining a time when there was nothing but the Waters of Chaos. In some stories the first thing to emerge from the waters is a blue lotus whose petals hide the infant sun god. Others start with the Primeval Mound, the first dry land, rising above the waters. To the mound comes a phoenix or a hawk or a goose called the Great Cackler who lays the world egg.

In another version a Creator god exists in the dark waters of chaos for countless ages before realizing that he is lonely. "With the thoughts of his heart and the words of his mouth" the Creator made gods and goddesses. Next he created a world with Egypt at its center. The first people were formed from the tears of the Creator. The Creator is sometimes identified with the sun god and sometimes with other important gods such as Ptah or Amon.

Egyptian gods and goddesses (deities) were all forms of the Creator but they took on identities of their own. Some had special areas

△ Written on papyrus, questions about when to sow seed, are put to the gods Sobek and Isis.

of interest: Thoth was god of wisdom and writing, Hathor a goddess of love and death.

Strange and sacred creatures

The deities were often shown in human form wearing distinctive headdresses and carrying sacred symbols. Some deities had several forms. The god Sobek could appear as a crocodile or as a man with the head of a crocodile. The goddess Hathor might be shown as a beautiful woman, as the head of a woman with cow's ears, as a cow or as a cow-headed woman. The sun god had numerous forms, some of them worshiped as separate gods. The rising sun was Khepri, shown as a scarab-beetle, the noonday sun was Horus, the hawk god, and the setting sun was Atum, shown as a ram-headed man.

Late in Egyptian history the cult of sacred animals became very important. Creatures such as the ibises sacred to Thoth or the crocodiles sacred to Sobek lived in temples and were given elaborate burials when they died.

▷ Granite statue of the god Horus as a crowned hawk, one of three still guarding entrances in the temple of Horus at Edfu. Real hawks were kept in a nearby grove. Every year one of these birds was chosen to be a living divine image in the temple of the Sacred Hawk, which once stood near the main temple.

Egyptian temples – palaces of the gods

A temple was the palace of the deity who lived in the cult statue. The statue was hidden inside a shrine in the sanctuary, the holiest part of the temple. Every morning the chief priest entered the sanctuary and opened the shrine. Many rituals were performed, including clothing and perfuming the statue and presenting a meal. In return for these offerings the gods were asked to keep Egypt safe and prosperous.

Ordinary people could not watch the daily ritual but they did join in festivals. At these, divine statues were carried outside the temple so the gods might "speak" to the people. Some temples were centers of learning and artists and craftsmen made a wide range of goods in temple workshops.

The major temples were state-controlled so the goods were distributed by the government. Kings gave estates, ships and slaves to support temples. In the 12th century BC the temple of Amon at Karnak had over 100,000 people working for it.

◁ ▷ Human and semi-human forms of some of the chief Egyptian deities:
1 *Horus*, son of Osiris, a sky god closely connected with the king.
2 *Set*, enemy of Horus and Osiris, god of storms and disorder.
3 *Thoth*, a moon deity and god of writing, counting and wisdom.
4 *Khnum*, a ram god who shapes men and their *kas* on his potter's wheel.
5 *Hathor*, goddess of love, birth and death.
6 *Sobek*, the crocodile god, Lord of the Faiyum.
7 *Ra*, the sun god in his many forms.
8 *Amon*, a creator god often linked with Ra.
9 *Ptah*, another creator god and the patron of craftsmen.
10 *Anubis*, god of mummification.
11 *Osiris*, god of agriculture and ruler of the dead.
12 *Isis*, wife of Osiris, mother of Horus and Mistress of Magic.

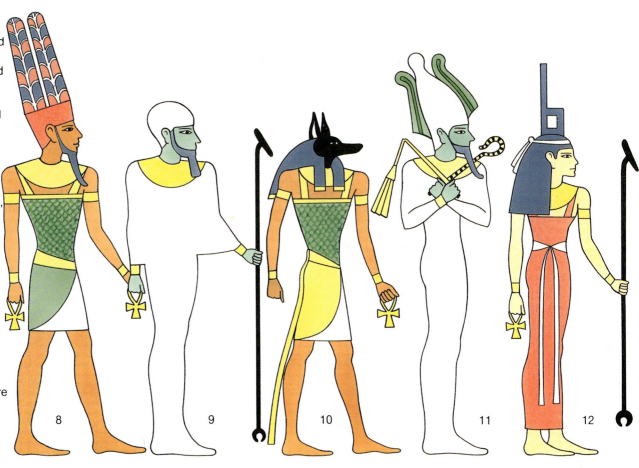

8   9   10   11   12

SCRIBES AND WRITING

Being able to read and write was essential for a career in the Egyptian civil service. Not much is known about Egyptian schools. Some temples ran schools but many boys seem to have studied with local scribes (trained writers).

Reading, writing and mathematics were the basic subjects. Pupils learned by copying out texts in the two main scripts, hieroglyphic and hieratic. They wrote with pens made from reeds on wooden tablets, pieces of pottery or scraps of papyrus. Surviving school texts show pupils' spelling mistakes and teachers' corrections. Discipline was strict: *"A boy's ear is in his back, he listens when he is beaten."*

Be a scribe!

Some of the texts that boys were made to copy out were about the advantages of being a scribe. They stress that scribes sit in the shade and watch while other people do the hard work. Wealth and success is promised to the good pupil. The texts conclude *"If you have any sense, you will be a scribe!"*

Scribes were employed to write official or private letters and to draw up legal documents. Other common tasks were recording the progress of all kinds of work and making lists of goods. Educated people read for pleasure so scribes wrote or copied out literature such as proverbs, stories and love poems.

△ This hieroglyph shows scribal equipment: a palette with cakes of red and black ink, a water pot and a papyrus smoother.

◁ A scribe's palette, from about 1800 BC, with four cakes of ink and a slot to hold reed pens. The ink was mixed with water.

△ A letter written on papyrus. It dates to about 2002 BC. The intact seal at the bottom shows that the letter never reached its destination. The name of the official it was meant for is written in hieratic. The same name written in hieroglyphic is shown alongside.

△ The Egyptians invented writing paper. This paper was made from the pith of *Cyperus papyrus*, a common marsh plant. The tall stems were cut down and carried off in bundles.

△ Each stem was stripped of its rind and cut into short pieces. These pieces were then cut lengthwise into narrow strips. It was essential to keep the papyrus pith moist.

△ ▷ Two layers of strips at right angles were put on a hard surface and beaten until they fused. The papyrus sheets were polished and then glued together to make scrolls.

◁ The hieroglyphic script at its most beautiful. These painted hieroglyphs are in a Theban tomb of c.1450 BC. The text, written in columns reading from right to left, tells how the owner enjoyed hunting.

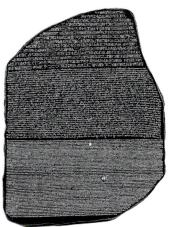

Hieroglyphic and other scripts

The hieroglyphic script was mainly for royal or religious texts carved in stone. Simplified (cursive) hieroglyphs were used for writing religious texts on papyrus. Letters, records, textbooks and literature were written in hieratic, a kind of shorthand hieroglyphic. In the 7th century BC an even more abbreviated script called demotic was introduced.

The hieroglyphic script has about 750 signs. Most are pictures of people, animals, plants or objects. There are two main types of sign – sound-signs and sense-signs. Sound-signs can represent from one to four consonants. The vowels were not written out. A sense-sign can be used to write a word or placed after a word to show the area of meaning. For example, verbs of motion have a pair of legs attached.

△ The Rosetta Stone dates to 196 BC. It is inscribed with a royal decree written in Egyptian in two different scripts, hieroglyphic and demotic, and in Greek. This helped the French scholar J-F. Champollion to decipher the hieroglyphic script.

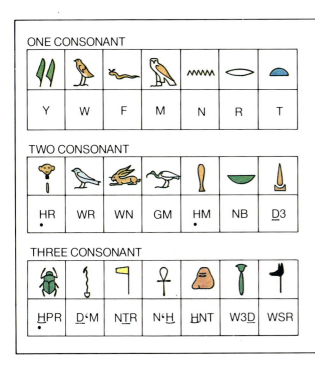

ONE CONSONANT

Y	W	F	M	N	R	T

TWO CONSONANT

HR	WR	WN	GM	HM	NB	D3

THREE CONSONANT

HPR	D'M	NTR	N'H	HNT	W3D	WSR

◁▷ A typical sentence in ancient Egyptian and a selection of sound-signs and sense-signs:

"His Majesty set out on a chariot of gold." This sentence comes from the Battle Annals of Thutmose III (see page 41). The transcription underneath shows which sound-signs are written by the hieroglyphs. The English translation below that follows the Egyptian word order. There are no breaks between words in Egyptian scripts. Marks under letters indicate pronunciation.

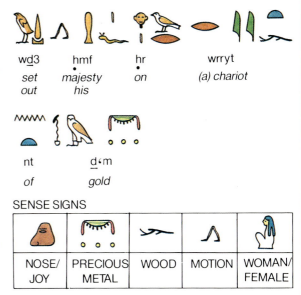

wd3	hmf	hr	wrryt
set out	majesty his	on	(a) chariot

nt	d'm
of	gold

SENSE SIGNS

NOSE/ JOY	PRECIOUS METAL	WOOD	MOTION	WOMAN/ FEMALE

BURIAL CUSTOMS

The ancient Egyptians took many precautions to make sure that the spirits of the dead could enjoy a life after death. Those who could afford them had elaborate family tombs.

People visited these tombs to make regular food offerings to their dead relations. In case the family neglected this duty, stone stelae (carved "gravestones") were placed in the outer areas of tombs. These often show the dead person sitting next to a table of food offerings. They are inscribed with a magical formula. The idea was that when this was spoken aloud the dead got everything they needed to live on.

The Book of the Dead

Before the dead could reach the paradise known as the Field of Reeds they had to pass through an underworld full of monsters and demons. In the Middle Kingdom some coffins were painted with maps of the underworld and with spells against its dangers. In the New Kingdom the spells were written on papyrus scrolls and placed in the tomb.

One spell collection known as the Book of the Dead stresses that all spirits were judged before Osiris. The dead person's heart was weighed against a feather representing *maat* – truth. If their heart was heavier than truth because they had led a wicked life they would be eaten by a monster and die a second death. Those who passed the judgment became blessed spirits who lived with the gods. Such spirits were still believed to want intact bodies to return to.

In early times burial in hot dry sand preserved bodies naturally. When coffins came into use some artificial way of stopping decay was needed. At some periods the process of mummification was used to preserve bodies.

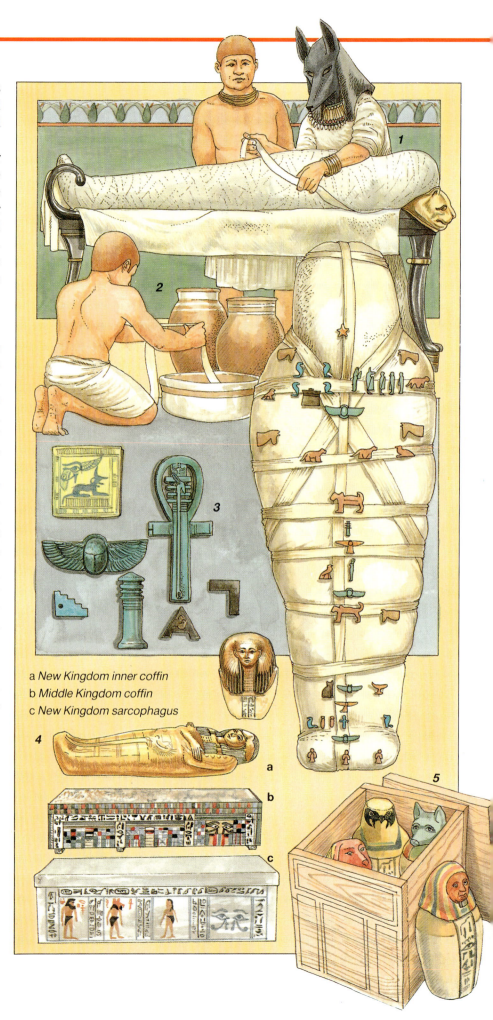

a *New Kingdom inner coffin*
b *Middle Kingdom coffin*
c *New Kingdom sarcophagus*

▷ Embalmers and burial equipment.
1 Wrapping a mummy. The chief embalmer wears a jackal mask to impersonate Anubis, protector of the dead.
2 Spells were recited as each part of the mummy was separately wrapped in long strips of linen. A shroud might then be tied over the whole mummy.
3 Amulets were placed in the layers of wrappings to protect each part of the body.
4 In richer burials the mummy might be placed in a set of cartonnage coffins inside a sarcophagus of stone. Cartonnage was made by soaking linen or papyrus layers in plaster.
5 The liver, lungs, stomach and intestines were packed into jars and placed near the coffin.

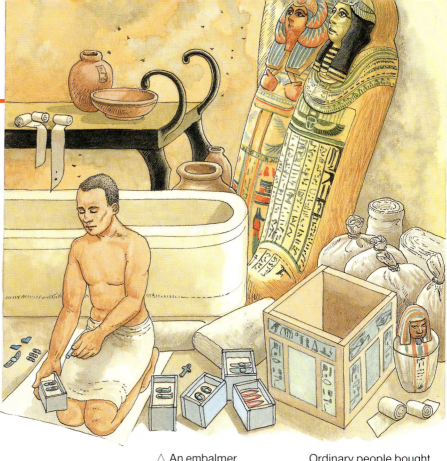

Mummification

The exact treatment depended on what the family could afford. The most elaborate method took about 70 days. First the embalmers took the brain out through the nose. The vital organs were removed and treated separately, though the heart might be left in the chest. The inside of the body was cleaned and packed with scented resins. Natron, a natural drying agent, was put inside and all around the body.

After about 40 days the body would have completely dried out. The next stage was to put packing material under the skin to imitate flesh and to refill the main cavity with scented materials. Finally the mummy was treated with perfumed oils and molten resin before being wrapped for burial.

△ An embalmer assembles a set of mummy amulets in a workshop full of funerary equipment. Decorated tombs and coffins were status symbols in ancient Egypt, sometimes given by the king to valued officials.

Ordinary people bought the best equipment they could afford in preparation for their own funerals. Personal possessions such as clothes, jewelry and furniture might also be buried with the dead for use in the afterlife.

△ The 3,300-year-old head of Seti I. This is the best preserved of all the royal mummies. Egyptian mummies give valuable information about the diseases people suffered from in ancient times.

▷ From about 1700 BC onwards magical figurines known as *shabtis* were placed in tombs. A *shabti* acted as a substitute for the tomb owner if his spirit was called up to do farm work in the afterlife.

◁ The shrouded mummy of a priestess in her anthropoid (mummy-shaped) coffin. The lid incorporates a mummy mask and painted garlands.

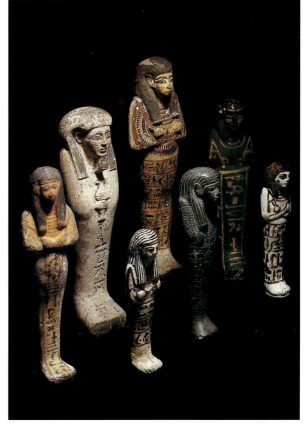

EVERYDAY LIFE

Most people in ancient Egypt were employed by the state, which also often provided them with housing. Wages were paid in the form of food, clothing and other necessities. Surplus rations could be swapped for household items and luxuries. These might be exchanged in their turn. In one typical transaction a New Kingdom workman bartered two goats, one pig and two planks of sycamore wood for a decorated coffin.

Food and drink
Bread, beer, vegetables and a little fresh or dried fish was the diet of the poor. Better-off Egyptians enjoyed dates, pomegranates and figs. They ate meat, especially beef and goose, and drank date or grape wine. Decayed teeth of some mummies suggest over-indulgence in cakes sweetened with honey and fruit.

Clothing and fashion
Most clothes were made of pleated linen. Men dressed in loincloths and kilts and, at some periods, shirts. Women had shawls and narrow ankle-length dresses. Reed or leather sandals might be worn outdoors. Children wore no clothes and had all but one side-lock of hair shaved off.

Adult hairstyles could be very elaborate, and important people owned wigs in a range of lengths and styles. Both sexes wore jewelry and used make-up, especially eye paint. The Egyptians loved perfume, and scented oils were rubbed into the skin.

▷ A tomb scene of craftsmen at work. At the top are leather-workers and men making burial items. In the 2nd row are chariot-makers, sculptors and carpenters. The 3rd row shows furniture and statues being finished off. In the 4th row are metal-workers and boat-builders.

▽ Left: A child's pull-along wooden horse, dating from the Greco-Roman periods. Right: A wooden comb, c.1300 BC, from Kom Medinet Ghurab. Many charming objects linked with hairdressing and make-up have survived from New Kingdom Egypt.

◁ Town life in ancient Egypt. Houses were made from mud brick. The homes of ordinary people were small and built close together. Livestock such as goats and geese might be kept in the middle of towns. Cats, dogs and monkeys were popular pets. Cooking was done in domed clay ovens in open kitchen-yards. The flat roofs were used as storage and work space.

EGYPT BEFORE THE PHARAOHS

The first inhabitants of Egypt were nomadic hunter-gatherers who lived on the savannah. Gradually people moved down into the Nile valley and adopted a settled way of life based on agriculture (see pages 10-11). We know very little about the way these people lived but there were separate groups with different cultures.

Predynastic peoples: Middle and Lower Egypt

Sometime around 5500 BC one group settled in an area centered on the Faiyum, a large lake in the middle of Egypt. This group did grow some crops but fishing seems to have been vital to their survival. Other groups, known from large village sites in Lower Egypt, grew corn, hunted desert animals and fished.

At Merimda Beni Salama, the earliest of the northern sites, people lived in clusters of reed huts. They used stone tools, made simple pottery and spun cloth. At the later site of Ma'adi there is evidence for farming, herding and metalworking.

Predynastic peoples: Upper Egypt

In the south the Badarian culture spread along the Nile valley. These people lived in small villages on the floodplain and buried their dead with grave-goods in cemeteries on the edge of the desert. This suggests a religion with a belief in an afterlife. Items found in Badarian graves include decorated pots, bead necklaces, linen clothing, clay figurines of people and animals, amulets, ivory spoons and combs.

Descended from the Badarian people was the Naqada I (or Amratian) culture. Metal was still rare but stone-working was highly skilled. Flint was worked into rippled knives and arrowheads and harder stones were made into clubs. These weapons would have been used for hunting the desert animals that were an important source of food. They may also indicate a more warlike society.

In the Naqada II (or Gerzean) Period people lived in large tribal communities that were probably often warring. Some burials contain much richer grave-goods than average such as gold and lapis lazuli jewelry, elaborate slate palettes used for grinding eye paint, and beautiful ivory combs and knife handles. This suggests a wealthy ruling class at this time.

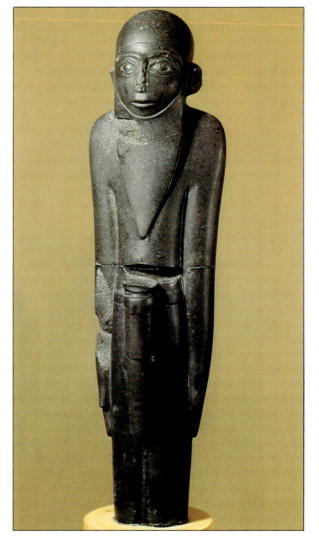

▽ A basalt statue (15in high) from Naqada, probably of the late Predynastic Period. This fine piece shows that the Egyptians had already mastered the art of carving in hard stone.

▽ Clay figure of a roaring hippopotamus from a Naqada II grave at Hiw. Hippopotamuses would have been a common danger in the Nile at this period. Hippopotamus hunts are shown on Predynastic pottery and hippopotamus tusks were carved into figurines and pendants.

◁ A crude clay figurine of a woman, from a tomb of the Naqada I Period. The exaggerated thighs and legs imply that the figurine was a fertility charm.

Trade in the Early Dynastic Period

A few Naqada II objects are decorated with motifs borrowed from the art of Mesopotamia (modern Iraq). A sophisticated urban society already existed in Mesopotamia at this date.

Some archaeologists believe that the rapid changes which took place in the Late Naqada II and Early Dynastic Periods were due to foreigners invading from the east and seizing power. There is no strong evidence for an invasion, but the Egyptians were certainly trading goods and ideas with the peoples to the east. It was probably at this time that the Upper Egyptians began mining and exporting gold. The important town of Ombos, near Naqada, was close to a major gold-mining area.

By the end of the Naqada II Period all of Upper Egypt was ruled by a line of chieftains who called themselves kings.

Major Predynastic and Early Dynastic sites

All dates given for the Predynastic cultures are uncertain. The cultures of Upper and Lower Egypt cannot easily be related in their development.

1 Badarian sites c.4500-4000 BC.
2 Naqada I sites c.4000-3500 BC.
3 Naqada II sites c.3500-3000 BC.
4 Lower Egypt cultures sites c.4800-3000 BC.
5 Faiyum "A culture" sites c.5500-4200 BC.
6 Late Naqada II and Early Dynastic sites c.3000-2575 BC.

△ A Naqada I red-ware pot decorated with desert animals, a frequent theme in the art of this period. The tombs near Naqada were excavated in 1895 by archaeologists.

▷ Predynastic and Early Dynastic Egypt. Most of the major Predynastic sites are on the margins of the desert. By Early Dynastic times many of these sites had been abandoned and new settlements were founded on the Nile's floodplain. In this period Nubia was inhabited by a people whom historians call the "A-Group."

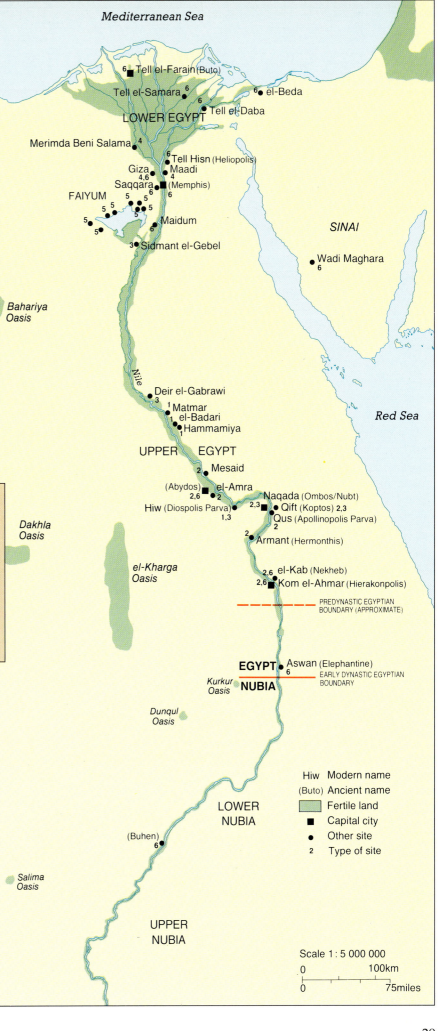

Mediterranean Sea

6 Tell el-Farain (Buto)
Tell el-Samara 6
6 el-Beda
6 Tell el-Daba
LOWER EGYPT
Merimda Beni Salama 4
6 Tell Hisn (Heliopolis)
Giza 4,6
Maadi 4
Saqqara (Memphis)
6
FAIYUM 5 5
5 5
5 5 5
5 Maidum
5 6
5 3 Sidmant el-Gebel

SINAI

Wadi Maghara
6

Bahariya Oasis

Red Sea

Nile

Deir el-Gabrawi
3
1 Matmar
1 el-Badari
1 Hammamiya

UPPER EGYPT

2 Mesaid
(Abydos) 2,6 2 el-Amra
Hiw (Diospolis Parva) 1,3
Naqada (Ombos/Nubt)
2,3 2 Qift (Koptos) 2,3
Qus (Apollinopolis Parva)
2 2
Armant (Hermonthis)
2,6 el-Kab (Nekheb)
2,6 Kom el-Ahmar (Hierakonpolis)

PREDYNASTIC EGYPTIAN BOUNDARY (APPROXIMATE)

Dakhla Oasis

el-Kharga Oasis

EGYPT Aswan (Elephantine)
6
Kurkur Oasis NUBIA
EARLY DYNASTIC EGYPTIAN BOUNDARY

Dunqul Oasis

Hiw Modern name
(Buto) Ancient name
▪ Fertile land
▪ Capital city
● Other site
2 Type of site

LOWER NUBIA

(Buhen) 6

Salima Oasis

UPPER NUBIA

Scale 1 : 5 000 000
0   100km
0   75miles

29

THE FIRST PYRAMID BUILDERS

According to Egyptian legend, the country was first united under a King Menes. Menes is said to have been a king of Upper Egypt who conquered Lower Egypt and founded a new capital at Memphis. Two early kings called Narmer and Aha, whose tombs were found in the sacred city of Abydos, have each been identified as Menes. Events from the reigns of both kings may have contributed to the legend of Menes and the founding of the 1st Dynasty.

Early Dynastic Egypt – an era of change

During the 1st Dynasty the use of writing became widespread. The idea of writing may have come from Mesopotamia but the Egyptians developed a unique pictorial script known as hieroglyphic (see pages 22-23).

Towns of some size were now established and brick buildings replaced reed huts. Brick *mastaba* tombs were built for high officials at Saqqara, the cemetery for Memphis. Inside these large rectangular flat-topped tombs, close to the burial chamber, were storerooms full of goods. Stone *stelae* were set up against one wall of the *mastaba* tomb at the place where offerings were made to the dead. When a ruler of this period died some of his servants were killed and buried near him so that their spirits could continue to serve him in the afterlife.

Selected Kings 1 – The Early Dynastic Period 2920-2575 BC

1st Dynasty 2920-2770
Menes (=Aha ?)
Djer
Djet
Den
Semerkhet
2nd Dynasty 2770-2649
Hetepsekhemwy   Ninetjer
Reneb   Peribsen
        Khasekhemwy

◁ King Djoser, builder of the Step Pyramid. This statue was found in a sealed chamber near the northeast corner of the pyramid.

3rd Dynasty 2649-2575
Nebka 2649-2630
Djoser 2630-2611
Sekhemkhet 2611-2603
Khaba 2603-2599
Huni 2599-2575

Little is known about the history of Early Dynastic Egypt. During the 2nd Dynasty there seems to have been a civil war between two kings, Peribsen and Khasekhemwy. These kings were followers of the rival gods Set and Horus. The victor, Khasekhemwy, included both gods in the writing of his full name (see page 18), perhaps as a gesture towards peace.

Khasekhemwy is the earliest Egyptian king we have stone statues of. All the royal mastaba tombs of the 1st and 2nd Dynasties have been robbed but the few objects that survive are very fine. Among them are four bracelets of gold, lapis lazuli and turquoise found in the tomb of King Djer at Abydos. They were on an arm torn from a mummy by tomb robbers.

▽ Limestone gaming disc decorated with a pair of owls. This disc is one of a set of 45 found in a Ist-Dynasty official's tomb. Board games were a popular pastime.

△ The restored south-east entrance to the Step Pyramid complex at Saqqara. These stone walls imitate the paneled brick of palaces of this period. Inside the enclosure was an area dedicated to Sed festivals (see page 16) at which Djoser could gain eternal life and power.

The genius Imhotep and the Step Pyramid

The reign of King Djoser in the 3rd Dynasty was later remembered as a golden age of wisdom. Among Djoser's officials was Imhotep, the first genius known to history.

Imhotep is said to have written books on medicine and was later worshiped as a god of healing. Tradition also named Imhotep as the inventor of stone architecture and the designer of Egypt's first pyramid – the Step Pyramid at Saqqara, built for King Djoser. Imhotep's name has been found in the Step Pyramid complex so he probably was the chief architect of this extraordinary group of stone buildings.

Like the later pyramids (see pages 86-87), the Step Pyramid complex was both a royal tomb and a temple where the spirit or *ka* of the dead king could be worshiped. Parts of it are stone versions of the temporary reed shrines of the Sed festivals. The effort and cost that went into building the Step Pyramid shows the importance of the cult of the divine king.

▽ The Step Pyramid at Saqqara – the first pyramid to be built – was begun in about 2630 BC. This makes it the oldest stone structure of its size in the world. Under the pyramid is the tomb of Djoser. This was robbed in ancient times and the granite sarcophagus was found empty.

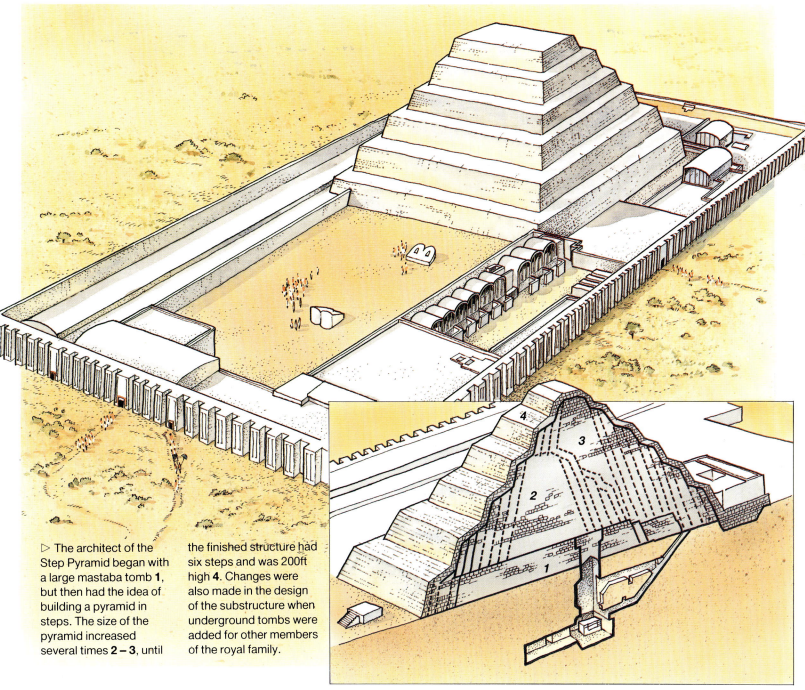

▷ The architect of the Step Pyramid began with a large mastaba tomb **1**, but then had the idea of building a pyramid in steps. The size of the pyramid increased several times **2 – 3**, until the finished structure had six steps and was 200ft high **4**. Changes were also made in the design of the substructure when underground tombs were added for other members of the royal family.

THE OLD KINGDOM

Snofru, the first king of the 4th Dynasty, built at least two true (straight-sided) pyramids for himself. One of these is known as the Bent Pyramid because half-way up its height it changes angle sharply.

During the 4th Dynasty the most important government posts were held by members of the royal family. In Snofru's reign the Egyptians built a fortified town at Buhen in Nubia. From here they could exploit the Nubian gold fields and control trade routes into Africa.

Snofru was reputed to be a kindly ruler. In contrast, Khufu (Cheops), the builder of the Great Pyramid at Giza, was long remembered as a cruel tyrant. Khephren and Menkaura also built vast pyramids at Giza.

The tombs of queens, princesses and high officials were grouped around the pyramids. Human sacrifice (see page 30) no longer had any part in the royal burial rites. Statues of 4th Dynasty kings show them as serene figures, confident in their power over Egypt and in their status as living gods. This may be misleading, as the brief reigns of some Old Kingdom rulers suggest conflicts we know little about.

The Old Kingdom was an intellectual high point. The best Egyptian medical and dental textbooks were written then. Mathematics, astronomy and engineering also flourished. The challenge of pyramid building may have been the driving force behind such advances.

Pyramid building – the work force

The pyramids were built by a permanent workforce of craftsmen and peasants called up to work on royal projects during the months when the fields were flooded. As many as 100,000 men may have labored for over 20 flood seasons to build each pyramid. Building projects on such a gigantic scale needed a stable and prosperous country and a genius for organization. The huge civil service developed to cope with pyramid building remained a key feature of Egyptian civilization.

The 5th-Dynasty pyramids are smaller and some are inscribed on the inside with spells to help the king become a god in the afterlife. Several 5th-Dynasty rulers built magnificent stone temples for the sun god Ra, so Egypt was still wealthy enough to afford such large-scale building projects.

▽ A wooden statue of a 6th-Dynasty "Chief of the Royal Farmers."

▽ Painted limestone statue from Saqqara. Important people were often shown as scribes, sitting cross-legged with papyrus rolls on their laps.

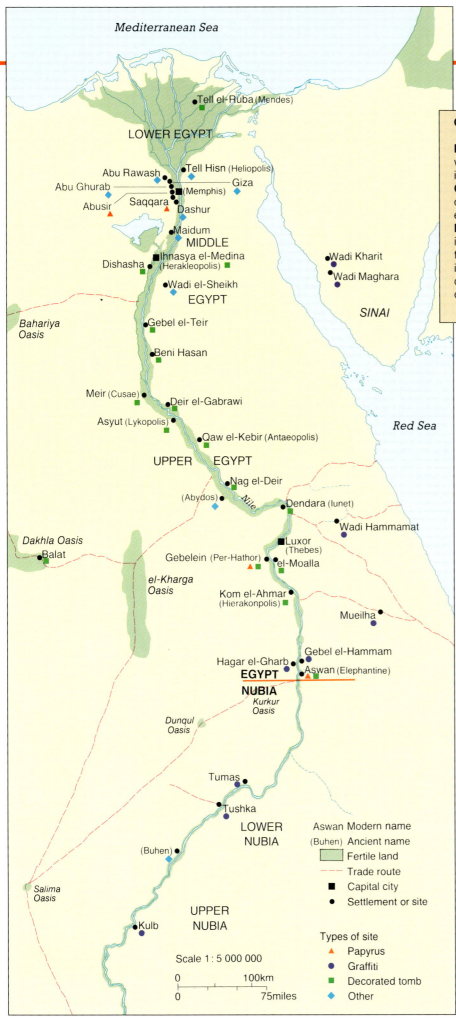

Old Kingdom and First Intermediate Period

Papyrus sites Papyrus was probably first used for writing on in the Old Kingdom. Old Kingdom papyri include legal documents and temple records.
Graffiti sites These consist of names and titles scratched on rocks by members of Egyptian mining and trading expeditions. Most are 6th-Dynasty.
Decorated tomb sites By the late Old Kingdom important officials were building themselves elaborate tombs in provincial cemeteries. This shows the increasing wealth and independence of the regions. The decoration in First Intermediate Period tombs is crude compared to Old Kingdom art.

Rise of the nomarchs

The 6th Dynasty brought a decline in royal power. The government was now no longer dominated by princes. In their wonderfully decorated tombs great officials hide their importance behind humble titles such as "Keeper of the King's Nail Clippings."

In theory all the land in Egypt belonged to the king but estates were given away to support temples and to reward officials. Such estates could be registered as belonging to the cults of gods or dead ancestors. This meant that little or no tax was payable on the produce of the estates and so the wealth of the king was cut down. The central government was also threatened by the gradual rise in power of the nomarchs (see pages 14–15). The office of nomarch had begun to pass from father to son.

The slide into chaos

The 6th Dynasty effectively ended with Pepy II who came to the throne as a small child and reigned for over 90 years. A series of low Niles caused famines, some nomarchs declared themselves kings and Egypt suffered what it feared most – chaos. The First Intermediate Period was a time of poverty and violence. The country's sufferings when central government failed became a common theme for later Egyptian writers *"All happiness has disappeared, the land is bowed down in misery."* (12th Dynasty poem).

◁ Egypt and Nubia in the Old Kingdom and the First Intermediate Period. The major 4th- and 5th-Dynasty sites are clustered near the capital, Memphis. Lower Nubia was almost uninhabited until it was settled by the "C-Group" during the 6th Dynasty.

33

THE MIDDLE KINGDOM

In 2040 BC Egypt was reunited by a king from Thebes, Nebhepetra Mentuhotpe. The country soon prospered and large-scale building works began again. After two more Theban kings a new dynasty, the 12th, was founded by the vizier Amenemhet. We do not know whether this transfer of power was peaceful or violent.

Amenemhet built a new capital city called Itjtawy somewhere near el-Lisht. After 20 years he made his son Senwosret co-ruler, an action copied by some later 12th-Dynasty kings. Amenemhet seems to have been murdered while Senwosret was away fighting the Libyans but there was no collapse of order. Under Amenemhet and Senwosret Egypt expanded into Nubia again and a long chain of forts was built along the Nile there.

The careworn kings

The greatest 12th-Dynasty king was Senwosret III. He conquered more of Nubia than the Egyptians had ever controlled before. Egyptian influence spread into Palestine. He also increased the power of the central government, at the expense of the nomarchs.

The pyramids of most 12th-Dynasty rulers were shoddily built but the art of this period is of a very high quality. Statues of Senwosret III and his son Amenemhet III show them with grim age-worn faces. They seem far more human than the god-kings of the previous era. Middle Kingdom literature, too, stresses the cares and problems of kingship.

Selected Kings 3 – Middle Kingdom 2040-1640 BC

11th Dynasty 2040-1991
Nebhepetra Mentuhotpe 2061-2010
Mentuhotpe II 2010-1998
Mentuhotpe III 1998-1991
12th Dynasty 1991-1783
Amenemhet I 1991-1962
Senwosret I 1971-1926
Amenemhet II 1929-1892
Senwosret II 1897-1878
Senwosret III 1878-1841
Amenemhet III 1844-1797
Amenemhet IV 1799-1787
Queen Nefrusobek 1787-1783
13th Dynasty 1783-1640
About 70 kings, most with short reigns. Among the best known are:
Sobekhotpe I c.1750
Hor c.1748 ?
Sobekhotpe III c.1745
Neferhotep I c.1741-1730
Sobekhotpe IV c.1730-1720
Sobekhotpe V c.1720-1715
Aya c.1704-1690
Neferhotep III
14th Dynasty
Minor kings contemporary with Dynasties 13 and 15.

15th Dynasty 1640-1532
Hyksos kings ruling from Avaris:
Salitis
Sheshi
Khian
Apophis c.1585-1542
Khamudi c.1542-1532
16th Dynasty
Minor Hyksos kings contemporary with the 15th Dynasty.
17th Dynasty 1640-1550
Numerous Theban kings, the best known are:
Inyotef V c.1640-1635
Seqenenra c.1560-1555
Kamose 1555-1550

◁ Seated figure in black basalt, a portrait of King Neferhotep I.

▽ A group of 40 model soldiers from a tomb at Asyut. The soldiers carry copper-headed spears and cowhide shields. Wooden models of scenes from daily life have been found in many Middle Kingdom tombs. Among the most common are boating, brewing and baking scenes.

◁ A beautifully carved granite obelisk of Senwosret I at Heliopolis. Obelisks were sacred to the sun god. Not much stone architecture survives from the Middle Kingdom.

The reign of the Hyksos

The 12th Dynasty ended with a queen, so the royal family had probably died out. Egypt continued to prosper in the 13th Dynasty but most kings only seem to have reigned for a few years. It is possible that real power was in the hands of officials such as the vizier. In time, rival dynasties emerged. One of these, the 15th, were foreigners known as the Hyksos.

The Hyksos people had entered Egypt through Palestine and settled in the Delta. These Hyksos kings managed to assert their power over the whole of Egypt. They also made an alliance with Kush, an area of Upper Nubia ruled by local princes.

During what is known as the Second Intermediate Period, local rulers were tolerated as long as they paid tribute to the Hyksos kings at their capital, Avaris. A new dynasty of Theban kings arose in the south. At first these 17th-Dynasty kings had to pay tribute to the Hyksos but their aim was to free Egypt from foreign control. King Seqenenra led an army against the Hyksos but the terrible axe wounds on his mummy show that he died after a battle. His successor, Kamose, continued the struggle, fighting the Hyksos and the Nubians of Kush.

▷ Egypt and Nubia in the Middle Kingdom and the Second Intermediate Period. The map shows capital cities and changing centers of power during the 11th to 17th Dynasties. These include areas of Nubia controlled by Egypt's line of forts along the Nile, and major sites of the Nubian culture groups.

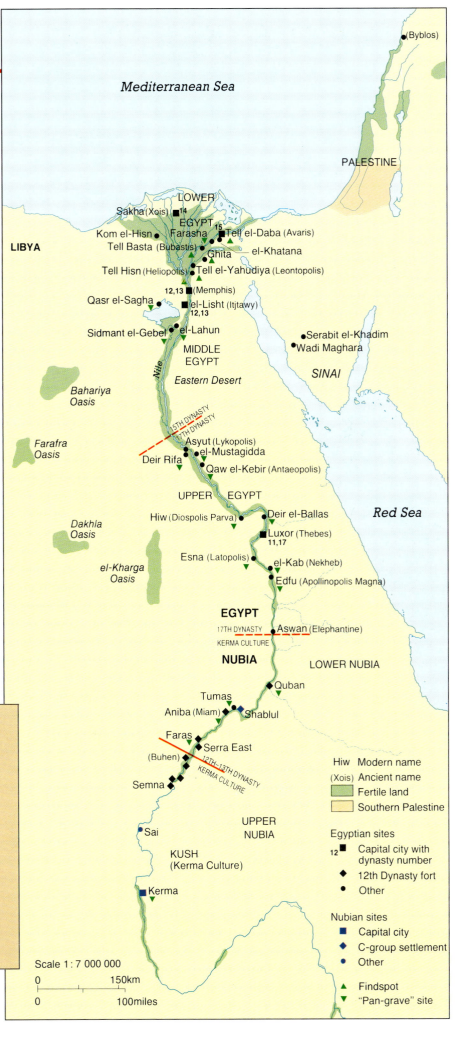

Middle Kingdom and Second Intermediate Period

Find spots The finds include bronze weapons and distinctive pottery of the Middle Bronze Age culture of Palestine and those parts of Egypt settled by the Hyksos.
Dynasty capitals The centers of power often changed with dynasties. The local god of a dynastic capital then became an important deity.
"Pan-grave" sites The "Pan-grave" people were nomads from the Eastern Desert who served as mercenary soldiers in Egypt and Nubia.
12th-Dynasty forts and "C-group" settlements The Egyptians built forts to control the "C-group" culture people of Lower Nubia and to create a buffer-zone against the fierce "Kerma culture" people of Kush (Upper Nubia). In the Second Intermediate Period the Princes of Kush ruled Lower Nubia.

THE NEW KINGDOM

Ahmose, first king of the 18th Dynasty, finally drove the Hyksos out of Egypt and the Prince of Kush out of Lower Nubia. By the end of his reign Egypt controlled an area from Palestine to Upper Nubia.

Thutmose I led the armies of Egypt further north than they had ever gone before and founded an empire in Palestine and Syria.

Thutmose II died young. His widow and sister, Hatshepsut, acted as regent for the boy king Thutmose III, her husband's son by a lesser wife. After a few years she declared herself king. Statues show her in male royal dress. Hatshepsut's reign seems to have been peaceful and prosperous. Reliefs in her beautiful temple at Deir el-Bahri depict an expedition returning from Punt (Somalia) with valuable goods such as incense trees.

After Hatshepsut's death, Thutmose III fought many campaigns to secure Egypt's rule in Palestine and Syria. Tribute from the empire and gold from Nubia made Egypt the richest nation in the ancient world. The 18th-Dynasty kings used this wealth to build temples. The most favored god was Amon, whose temple at Karnak, Thebes, became the largest in Egypt.

Selected Kings 4 – New Kingdom 1550-1070 BC

18th Dynasty 1550-1070
Ahmose 1550-1525
Amonhotep I 1525-1504
Thutmose I 1504-1492
Thutmose II 1492-1479
Thutmose III 1479-1425
Queen Hatshepsut 1473-1458
Amonhotep II 1427-1401
Thutmose IV 1401-1391
Amonhotep III 1391-1353
Amonhotep IV (Akhenaten) 1353-1335
Smenkhkara (Queen Nefertiti?) 1335-1333

△ King Ramesses II shown as a sphinx – a human-headed lion.

Tutankhamon 1333-1323
Aya 1323-1319
Horemheb 1319-1307

19th Dynasty 1307-1196
Ramesses I 1307-1306
Seti I 1306-1290
Ramesses II 1290-1224
Merneptah 1224-1214
Seti II 1214-1204
Siptah 1204-1198
Queen Tawosre 1198-1196

20th Dynasty 1196-1070
Sethnakhte 1196-1194
Ramesses III 1194-1163
Ramesses IV 1163-1156
Ramesses V 1156-1151
Ramesses VI 1151-1143
Ramesses VII 1143-1136
Ramesses VIII 1136-1131
Ramesses IX 1131-1112
Ramesses X 1112-1100
Ramesses XI 1100-1070

▽ A riverside scene in the New Kingdom. The *shaduf*, shown lifting water from the river to irrigate an orchard, was a New Kingdom invention. An overseer standing on the bank is dressed in the elaborate costume of this period.

▷ Egypt and Nubia in the New Kingdom and the early Third Intermediate Period. During the latter period the High Priests of Amon at Thebes controlled the area between Aswan and el-Hiba while the kings of the 21st and 22nd Dynasties ruled the north. The sites marked in Nubia are towns or temples built by the Egyptians during the New Kingdom.

Mediterranean Sea

LOWER EGYPT

PALESTINE

Sa el-Hagar (Sais)
21,22 San el-Hagar (Tanis)
19,20 Tell el-Daba (Pi-Ramesses)
23 Tell el-Muqdam (Leontopolis)
22 Tell Basta (Bubastis)

Saqqara (Memphis) **18,19**

MIDDLE EGYPT

Kom Medinet Ghurab
Ihnasya el-Medina (Herakleopolis)

21ST-22ND DYNASTY HIGH PRIESTS OF AMON

el-Hiba (Ankyronon Polis)

Bahariya Oasis

Serabit el-Khadim

SINAI

el-Ashmunein (Hermopolis)
el-Amarna (Akhetaten) **18**

Red Sea

Nile

UPPER EGYPT

Dakhla Oasis

(Abydos)
Dendara (Iunet)
Qift (Koptos)

Deir el-Bahri
Luxor (Thebes) **18**

el-Kharga Oasis

el-Kab (Nekheb)
Edfu (Apollinopolis Magna)

EGYPT
NUBIA
Aswan (Elephantine)

Kurkur Oasis

Beit el-Wali

Dunqul Oasis

LOWER NUBIA

Aniba (Miam)
el-Lessiya
el-Sebua

Abu Simbel
Faras
(Buhen)
Mirgissa (Iqen)

Salima Oasis

Kumma

UPPER NUBIA

Sai
Soleb
Sesebi

Qift   Modern name
(Koptos) Ancient name
Fertile land
18 ■ Egyptian capital city with dynasty number
■ Nubian capital city
● Other Egyptian site

Scale 1 : 5 000 000

0   100km
0   75miles

Capital Cities of the New Kingdom and later

Thebes The New Kingdom religious capital and the royal burial place.
Memphis Administrative capital for the majority of the 18th Dynasty and in the early 19th Dynasty.
el-Amarna New capital begun in year 5 of Akhenaten. Abandoned some 15 years later under Tutankhamon.
Pi-Ramesses Built under Ramesses II. The probable site is the Qantir district near Tell el-Daba in the north-east of the Delta.
Tanis Capital and burial place of kings of the 21st and 22nd Dynasties.
Bubastis Capital and city of origin of the 22nd Dynasty in 945 BC.
Leontopolis Capital and probable burial place of some 23rd-Dynasty rulers.

Akhenaten, the Sun King

Amonhotep III built more lavishly than any of his predecessors. Remains of his palace at Thebes show the splendor and luxury of his court. His son, Amonhotep IV, changed his name to Akhenaten and made Aten (the sun disc) the chief deity of Egypt. He began to build a new capital at el-Amarna. Next he declared that Aten was the only god and closed down the temples of all the other deities. Akhenaten also broke with tradition by having himself shown in informal family scenes, kissing his beautiful wife Nefertiti (see page 18) or playing with his daughters. Akhenaten's reforms were not popular and in the reign of Tutankhamon the new capital was abandoned and the old religion was restored.

The Ramessid Pharaohs

After Tutankhamon the throne passed to a series of officials. The third was a general, Ramesses, who founded the 19th Dynasty. His son, Seti I, was a forceful ruler. His grandson, Ramesses II, reigned for 66 years and erected more buildings and colossal statues than any other Egyptian king.

Egypt was still prosperous but its borders were under threat. Merneptah, Ramesses II's successor, had to fight off Libyans and other invaders. Ramesses III, the second king of the 20th Dynasty, fought great land and sea battles against a group of invaders known as the Sea Peoples. The 20th Dynasty was a period of slow decline when the power of the priesthood at Thebes began to rival that of the king.

EGYPT & THE NEAR EAST

The Egyptians thought themselves superior to all other races. Foreigners usually appear in Egyptian art as humble tribute bearers or as bound prisoners. The Nubians to the south, the Libyans to the west and the "vile Asiatics" to the east were pictured on the king's footstool or on the underside of his sandals to symbolize Egypt trampling on its enemies. In reality some Near Eastern nations were dangerous rivals.

Legacy of the Hyksos

During the late Middle Kingdom large numbers of Asiatics were allowed to settle in Egypt. This seems to have made it easy for the Hyksos kings to seize power (see page 35). The Asiatic immigrants brought new bronze-working techniques and improved types of loom and potter's wheel. They also introduced new kinds of weapons and the practice of fighting from chariots.

The Theban kings of the 17th and 18th Dynasties were not content to drive the Hyksos out of Egypt. They pursued them into Palestine and southern Syria. These areas were divided into small states with ruling princes who could be terrorized into acknowledging the king of Egypt as their overlord and into paying him tribute. Northern Syria, however, was part of the powerful kingdom of Mitanni (Naharin).

Warrior kings against Mitanni and the Hittites

Thutmose I attacked Mitanni and led an Egyptian army as far north as the river Euphrates. He celebrated victory with a great elephant hunt at Niya.

To keep control of the empire it had won, Egypt frequently had to send an army to recapture rebel states or to threaten Mitanni. Thutmose III fought 14 major campaigns in Palestine and Syria. Inscriptions in the temple of Karnak record booty won on these campaigns and a relief shows exotic plants, birds and animals collected for the king in Syria.

Egypt and Mitanni eventually made peace. Thutmose IV and his son, Amonhotep III, both married princesses of Mitanni and sent gifts of gold in return. Under Akhenaten foreign affairs were neglected and parts of the empire broke away from Egyptian control.

By the 19th Dynasty Mitanni had declined and Egypt's chief rival in the Near East was the

△ The two-wheeled horse-drawn chariot was introduced into Egypt by the Hyksos. The Egyptians soon learned to use chariotry against their Near Eastern enemies.

▽ An 18th-Dynasty painting showing tribute bearers from Syria. The tribute includes fine gold vessels and a horn filled with perfumed oil. The child could be a slave or a hostage.

Hittite empire. The Hittites, a warlike people whose homeland was the mountains of Anatolia (now in modern Turkey, more than 600mi from Thebes) battled with Seti I and Ramesses II for control of Syria.

The battle of Qadesh was a personal victory for Ramesses II but a few years later he signed a peace treaty with the Hittites and married a Hittite princess. The Hittite empire was destroyed in the 12th century BC by the mass migration of the Sea Peoples (see also page 33). Egypt narrowly escaped being overwhelmed by the Sea Peoples and all of its Near Eastern empire was lost.

Northern Frontiers of the Egyptian Empire

1 Furthest point reached by Thutmose I.
2 Frontier at the end of Thutmose III's reign.
3 Frontier in year 7 of Amonhotep II.
4 Frontier under Thutmose IV.
5 Frontier under Tutankhamon.
6 Frontier in year 21 of Ramesses II.
Hittite empire The pink area shows the Hittite empire at its greatest extent. The capital was Hattusas, in the north.
Assyria The Assyrians rose in power after the decline of Mitanni.

▽ Egypt and the Near East (c.1530-1190 BC). Egypt traded with Cyprus, Crete and Mycenaean Greece.

The great Near Eastern powers were the Mitannis, Hittites, Babylonians and Assyrians.

Boğazköy (Hattusas)

HITTITE EMPIRE
ANATOLIA
(KIZZUWATNA)

Tell Fakariya (Washukanni) ?

GREECE (Mycenae)

Crete (Keftiu)   (Knossos)

CYPRUS (ALASHIYA)

Ras Shamra (Ugarit)
(Carchemish)
MITANNI (NAHARIN)
(Niya)
(Assur)

ASSYRIA

Euphrates
MESOPOTAMIA
Tigris

1
2
SYRIA
Qadesh
(Byblos)
3
4
5
Damascus
6

Mediterranean Sea

(Megiddo)

(Babylon)
BABYLON

PALESTINE

Gaza (Lachish)

LIBYA

San el-Hagar (Tanis)
Tell Basta (Bubastis)

(Memphis)
Timna

Serabit el-Khadim

el-Hiba (Ankyronon Polis)

el-Amarna (Akhetaten)

Nile

Karnak (Ipet-Isut)
Luxor (Thebes)

Red Sea

EGYPT Aswan (Elephantine)
NUBIA

Aniba (Miam)

(Buhen)

Gebel Barkal (Napata)

Aniba Modern name
(Miam) Ancient name
▨ Hittite empire c. 1370–1330BC
■ Capital city
● Other site
? Possible location

─2 Northern frontier of the Egyptian empire

Scale 1 : 13 000 000
0 ————— 400km
0 ————— 300miles

△ On this clay tablet, dating to 1355 BC, is a letter from King Tushratta of Mitanni to Amonhotep III of Egypt.

It is part of an archive of correspondence found at el-Amarna. It is written in cuneiform with an Egyptian translation, in the hieratic script, at the bottom. The letter is about a statue of the goddess Ishtar sent to Egypt to help cure Amonhotep III. The king's complaint may have been toothache as his mummy had dreadful tooth abscesses.

THE EGYPTIAN ARMY

The Egyptians do not seem to have been a very warlike people by nature. Egyptian accounts of the "ideal man" make little mention of qualities such as strength, courage or skill in battle.

There was no large permanent army in the Old Kingdom. Troops were mustered as the need arose. They were led by officials rather than by professional soldiers. Such troops seem to have spent more time on tasks like quarrying minerals in the desert than in fighting.

In the Middle Kingdom the army was larger, and fierce Nubian tribesmen were employed as mercenary soldiers. The great chain of fortresses built along the Nile to subdue Nubia needed permanent garrisons. At this period the army consisted of foot soldiers equipped with bows and arrows and copper-headed spears or axes. Other weapons used were copper daggers and wooden clubs and throwsticks. Large shields of stiffened cowhide were carried but no helmets or body armor were worn.

By the New Kingdom, Egypt had a large professional army using new or improved weapons. Stronger axheads and dagger blades were cast in bronze and the scimitar, a curved sword, came into use. A new type of bow had a greater range and power.

The charioteers – the king's elite force
From the 18th Dynasty onwards the army was divided into infantry and chariotry. The horse-drawn chariots were made of wood and leather and sometimes decorated with gold. They each carried two men: the charioteer who drove and the chariot-warrior who was armed with a bow and a spear or sword. Such warriors might wear a protective tunic of leather or bronze. In the early stages of a battle the chariot division would charge the enemy forces at great speed, with the chariot warriors firing off arrows. The chariotry was the elite of the Egyptian army, often led by the king in person.

▽ Ramesses II's army in camp. Chariot horses are tethered in rows to be fed and watered while close by a chariot is being repaired. A company of foot soldiers is drilled by its standard-bearer and the king's pet lion is being taken for a walk. None of the soldiers have helmets; thick wigs or bushy hairstyles cushioned the head from blows. The weapons shown include shields made of cowhide stretched on wooden frames and a bow made from two antelope horns lashed together.

Famous battles

Detailed accounts survive of some New Kingdom battles. The annals of Thutmose III at Karnak relate how the king led a surprise attack on the Palestinian city of Megiddo in 1456 BC. After a battle and short siege the city surrendered. Among the booty were 924 chariots and over 2,000 horses.

Even more is known about a battle fought between Ramesses II and the Hittite king Muwatallis in northern Syria in 1285 BC. Misled by false information, the Egyptians were ambushed as they set up camp close to the city of Qadesh. One division of the Egyptian army scattered in panic but Ramesses rallied his remaining troops and held off the enemy until reinforcements arrived. It is claimed in a poem that Ramesses fought this battle *"like a fierce lion in a valley of goats."* The king's courage turned a near disaster into an Egyptian victory. Losses were heavy on both sides.

▽ These details from the Battle of Qadesh are based on reliefs in temples built by Ramesses II.
Ramesses II's army had four main divisions named after Egyptian gods. The King was with Amon, the leading division, which set up camp near Qadesh not knowing that the Hittite army was hidden behind the city. The Ra division was attacked by the Hittite chariotry. It broke and fled. The Hittites chased it to the Egyptian camp. Ramesses and his guard fought their way through the Hittite lines towards the approaching Ptah division. After a fierce battle the Hittites retreated.

EGYPT DIVIDED

By the end of the 20th Dynasty Egypt had lost Nubia as well as its Near Eastern empire. The late 20th-Dynasty kings in their Delta capital had little influence over Upper Egypt. The High Priest of Amon, controller of the vast wealth of the temple of Karnak, was the effective ruler of the south. The office of High Priest was now always held by members of one family.

The Third Intermediate Period

On the death of the last 20th-Dynasty ruler, a king called Smendes claimed power in the north. At the start of the era known as the Third Intermediate Period the capital was Tanis in the northeastern Delta. The 21st-Dynasty kings brought statues, obelisks and decorated blocks from earlier reigns to adorn this city.

The dynasty of High Priests at Thebes acknowledged the claims of the 21st-Dynasty kings but continued to rule the south. Even in the Delta power was soon disputed.

Dynastic rivalries and attempts at unity

During the late New Kingdom large numbers of Libyans had settled in Lower Egypt and become a force there. A family of Libyan descent provided the first king of the 22nd Dynasty, Shoshenq I. He was a vigorous ruler who recovered a number of Egypt's former territories in Palestine.

By this time the Jews had established the kingdom of Judah. Shoshenq attacked Judah and carried off a great quantity of treasure from the temple at Jerusalem. His campaigns are recorded in the buildings he added to the temple of Karnak.

Shoshenq installed his own son as High Priest at Thebes so that all of Egypt was dominated by a single dynasty again. This fragile unity lasted for about a century. Then there were rebellions in the south and a rival dynasty, the 23rd, was established in the Delta. Egypt began to split up into small areas whose rulers called themselves kings. Two of the most important were the rulers of Hermopolis and Herakleopolis.

King Osorkon IV of the 23rd Dynasty tried to control the south by abolishing the now hereditary office of High Priest of Amon and making his daughter High Priestess instead. The High Priestess was supposed to be the

◁ The royal mask of Psusennes I, part of his silver coffin from Tanis.

Selected Kings 5 – The Third Intermediate Period 1070-712 BC	Osorkon I 984-978 Siamun 978-959 Psusennes II 959-945 **22nd Dynasty 945-712** Shoshenq I 945-924 Osorkon II 924-909 Takelot I 909-? Shoshenq II ?-883 Osorkon III 883-855
21st Dynasty 1070-945 Smendes 1070-1044 Amenemnisu 1044-1040 Psusennes I 1040-992 Amenemope 993-984	

Takelot II 860-835
Shoshenq III 835-783
23rd Dynasty c. 828-712
Rulers of Thebes, Hermopolis, Herakleopolis, Leontopolis and Tanis. The order of these kings is uncertain and some would have been contemporaries. They include:
Pedubaste I 828-803
Osorkon IV 777-749
Peftjauawybast 740-725
24th Dynasty 724-712
Rulers of Sais:
Tefnakhte 724-717
Bocchoris 717-712
25th Dynasty 770-712
Ruling Nubia and the Theban area:
Kashta 770-750
Piye 750-712
(25th-Dynasty kings continued on page 44)

△ A 22nd-Dynasty gold case containing a rolled strip of papyrus. On the papyrus is written a promise from the god Khons to protect the wearer.

bride of the god Amon. This meant that she could not marry a human husband and found a dynasty to rival the royal family.

Kings out of Nubia

All of Nubia was now ruled by the kings of Napata (see page 45). Though Nubian by birth, they had adopted Egyptian culture and religion. They built pyramids and were devoted to the worship of Amon. One of these 25th-Dynasty rulers, Kashta, gained power over the region between Aswan and Thebes.

Kashta's successor, Piye, invaded Egypt claiming that he was restoring order and the proper worship of the gods. Piye forced the High Priestess at Thebes to adopt his sister as her successor. He crushed the local ruler of Hermopolis and led his army as far north as Memphis. Tefnakhte, a chieftain who ruled the western Delta, was also forced to submit to Piye. The Nubian king then returned south, but his conquest of the north was temporary.

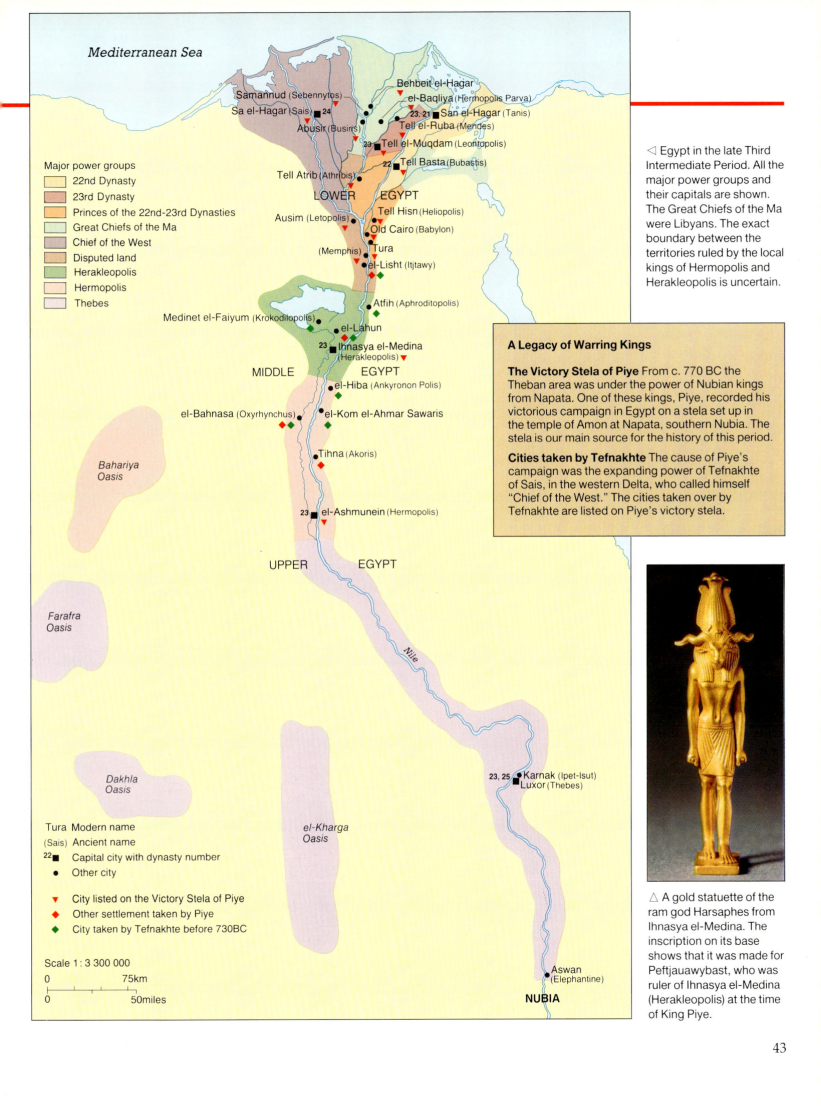

◁ Egypt in the late Third Intermediate Period. All the major power groups and their capitals are shown. The Great Chiefs of the Ma were Libyans. The exact boundary between the territories ruled by the local kings of Hermopolis and Herakleopolis is uncertain.

A Legacy of Warring Kings

The Victory Stela of Piye From c. 770 BC the Theban area was under the power of Nubian kings from Napata. One of these kings, Piye, recorded his victorious campaign in Egypt on a stela set up in the temple of Amon at Napata, southern Nubia. The stela is our main source for the history of this period.

Cities taken by Tefnakhte The cause of Piye's campaign was the expanding power of Tefnakhte of Sais, in the western Delta, who called himself "Chief of the West." The cities taken over by Tefnakhte are listed on Piye's victory stela.

△ A gold statuette of the ram god Harsaphes from Ihnasya el-Medina. The inscription on its base shows that it was made for Peftjauawybast, who was ruler of Ihnasya el-Medina (Herakleopolis) at the time of King Piye.

43

THE LAST EGYPTIAN RULERS

After Piye, the next 25th-Dynasty king was Shabaka. He defeated a king claiming to rule the Delta from Sais and destroyed all other opposition. Shabaka then ruled a united kingdom of Egypt and Napata from Memphis. Egypt prospered at this time but the whole of the Near East was entering a period of turmoil in which great empires rose and fell.

The Assyrian conquest of Egypt

In the 7th century BC the Assyrians were trying to extend their empire into Palestine. Egypt formed a defensive alliance with the kingdom of Judah. This angered the Assyrians. Their first attempt to invade Egypt was unsuccessful but then in 671 BC the Assyrian king Esarhaddon captured Memphis.

The 25th-Dynasty king Taharqa fled to Napata and Egypt was forced to pay tribute to the Assyrians. The local ruler of Sais, Necho, was allowed to call himself a king in return for serving the Assyrians. Necho was killed fighting Tantamani, the successor of Taharqa. The next Assyrian king, Assurbanipal, drove Tantamani back to Napata and sacked Thebes.

Necho's son, Psammetichus, was left as a puppet ruler in the Delta, but once trouble arose for the Assyrians in other parts of their empire

◁ This quartzite head is thought to be of King Amasis. In Egyptian stories he was remembered as a jovial man, fond of practical jokes.

**Selected Kings 6 –
The Late Period 712-332 BC**

25th Dynasty 712-657
Ruling Egypt and Nubia:
Shabaka 712-698
Shebitku 698-690
Taharqa 690-664
Tantamani 664-657
26th Dynasty 664-525
Kings from Sais:
Necho I 672-664
Psammetichus I 664-610
Necho II 610-595
Psammetichus II 595-589
Apries 589-570
Amasis 570-526
Psammetichus III 526-5
**27th Dynasty 525-404
(Ist Persian period)**
Cambyses 525-522
Darius I 521-486
Xerxes I 486-466
Artaxerxes I 465-424

Darius II 424-404
28th Dynasty 404-399
Amyrtaios 404-399
29th Dynasty 399-380
Nepherites I 399-393
Hakoris 393-380
30th Dynasty 380-343
Nectanebo I 380-362
Teos 365-360
Nectanebo II 360-343
2nd Persian Period
Artaxerxes III 343-338
Arses 338-336
Darius III 335-332
Period interrupted by a native ruler, Khababash

▷ An important priest shown as a scribe. In the Late Period artists often copied or adapted ideas from Old Kingdom art. This piece dates from about 650 BC but it was inspired by scribe statues made almost 2,000 years earlier.

◁ Bronze head of a hawk god. This head was probably attached to a wooden staff and carried in temple processions. Fine bronzes are a feature of Late Period art.

Mediterranean Sea

Samannud (Sebennytos)
Sa el-Hagar
(Sais) 26, 28
(Naukratis)
Tell el-Ruba (Mendes)
30
29 B
A
Kom Abu Billo (Terenuthis)
C D
Tell el-Farama (Pelusium)
Tell el-Muqdam (Leontopolis)
Tell el-Yahudiya
(Leontopolis)
Saqqara
(Memphis)
25

A Abusir (Busiris)
B San el-Hagar (Tanis)
C Tell Atrib (Athribis)
D Saft el-Hinna
(Per-Sopdu)

LOWER EGYPT

Nile-Red Sea Canal

Gaza
Jerusalem
(Jerusalem)
JUDAH
Dead
Sea

Ihnasya el-Medina
(Herakleopolis)

MIDDLE EGYPT

SINAI

Bahariya
Oasis

Farafra
Oasis

el-Ashmunein (Hermopolis)

Asyut (Lykopolis)

Nile

Dakhla
Oasis

Girga (Thinis)

(Hibis)
el-Kharga
Oasis

Red Sea

Karnak (Ipet-Isut)
Luxor (Thebes)

UPPER EGYPT

EGYPT
Aswan (Elephantine)
NUBIA

LOWER NUBIA

Karanog
Wadi el-Arab

Abu Simbel
Faras
(Buhen)

Semna

Firka

NAPATA-MEROE

Tabo
Kawa
Gebel Barkal
(Napata)
Nuri
el-Kurru
Debba

Kawa Modern name
(Sais) Ancient name
▨ Fertile land
● Stela of Darius
⟶ Route of Psammetichus' army

Egyptian sites
28 ■ Capital city with dynasty number
▼ City in Assurbanipal's annals
● Other

Nubian sites
■ Capital city
◆ Napata-Meroe

Begrawiya
(Meroe)

Wad Ban Naqa

Scale 1 : 7 000 000
0   150km
0   100miles

Saba

he managed to drive them out and make himself king of all Egypt.

War and peace – Egypt allies with Greece

Under the Saite kings of the 26th Dynasty art and literature flourished but Egypt was rarely at peace. Babylon became a greater power than Assyria. In 601 Necho II repelled an invasion by Nebuchadnezzar of Babylon. Psammetichus II led an army deep into Nubia to intimidate the ruler of Napata. The next king, Apries, was deposed by Amasis, an Egyptian general. By this time many Greeks were serving in the Egyptian army and Amasis encouraged a Greek trading settlement at Naukratis.

The Persian invasion

By the late 6th century BC Persia had become the main power in the Near East. In 525 BC the Persian ruler Cambyses conquered Egypt.

Cambyses shocked the ancient world by his brutality and his contempt for local deities. His successor, Darius I, was more humane but the Egyptians bitterly resented Persian rule. There were rebellions led by a series of Egyptian dynasties. None was successful for very long.

In the late 4th century BC the whole of the Persian empire was conquered by the young king of Macedon, Alexander the Great. When he arrived in Egypt he was hailed as a savior by the Egyptians.

Invasion and Conquest During the Late Period

The annals of Assurbanipal This Assyrian king left detailed records of his wars. He lists cities in Egypt whose rulers paid homage to him. These petty rulers are described as kings, showing how divided Egypt had become.
The route of Psammetichus' army The route probably taken by Psammetichus II when he invaded Napata in 591 BC. Evidence for the route comes from graffiti left by Psammetichus' army. Many of his soldiers were Greek mercenaries.
Stelae of Darius The Persian king Darius I completed a canal begun by Necho II. This canal linked a branch of the Nile to the Red Sea. Darius set up four stelae recording this achievement along the banks of the canal.

◁ Egypt and the kingdom of Napata-Meroe, united under Shabaka before the Assyrian conquest. Meroe became the Nubian capital c. 591 BC. The kingdom of Meroe endured until the 4th century AD.

EGYPT UNDER GREEK & ROMAN RULE

When Alexander the Great died in 323 BC his empire began to break up. A Macedonian general, Ptolemy, brought Alexander's body to Egypt and built a tomb for him in the new city of Alexandria in the Delta. In 304 BC Ptolemy declared himself king of Egypt. He and his descendents ruled Egypt for the next 250 years.

Scholars and artists were encouraged to come to Alexandria and Ptolemy established a great library there. Many Greeks and Macedonians were given grants of land in Egypt. The officials appointed by the Ptolemies were almost always Greek rather than Egyptian.

A murderous family

Ptolemaic kings usually married their sisters. These royal ladies often acted as co-rulers. There were frequent power struggles within the family and many Ptolemaic rulers seized or kept the throne by murdering close relations.

There were some rebellions against Greek rule in Upper Egypt. The Ptolemies tried to please their Egyptian subjects by building splendid temples to the Egyptian gods.

By the 1st century BC Rome had become the greatest power in the ancient world. The Romans wanted Egypt for its gold and grain.

**Selected Rulers 7 –
The Greco-Roman
Period 332 BC-AD 395**

**Macedonian Dynasty
332-304**
Alexander the Great
332-323
Philip Arrhidaeus 323-316
Alexander IV 316-304
**Ptolemaic Dynasty
304-30**
*The reigns of most later
Ptolemies were
interrupted by civil wars.*
Ptolemy I 304-284
Ptolemy II 285-246
Ptolemy III 246-221
Ptolemy IV 221-205
Ptolemy V 205-180
Ptolemy VI 180-164 &
163-145

Ptolemy VII 145
Ptolemy VIII 170-163 &
145-116

△ A coin of Cleopatra VII. The Egyptians had no coins until Greek rule.

Queen Cleopatra III &
Ptolemy IX 116-107
Queen Cleopatra III &
Ptolemy X 107-88
Ptolemy IX 88-81
Queen Cleopatra IV
81-80
Ptolemy XI 80
Ptolemy XII 80-58 &
55-51
Queen Berenice IV
58-55
Ptolemy XIII 51-47
Ptolemy XIV 47-44
Queen Cleopatra VII
51-30

**Roman rule
30 BC-AD 395**
*Rule by Prefects
appointed by the Emperor.*

Queen Cleopatra VII

In 48 BC the great Roman general Julius Caesar intervened in an Egyptian civil war to support Cleopatra as ruler. The first Ptolemy to learn Egyptian, Cleopatra captivated Julius Caesar by her wit and beauty. A son was born to them.

After Julius Caesar was murdered another Roman general, Mark Antony, fell in love with Cleopatra. Antony and Cleopatra ruled the east together until they were attacked by Julius Caesar's heir, Octavian (Augustus). Antony and Cleopatra were defeated and forced to take their own lives. Egypt became just another province of the Roman Empire.

△ Part of the ruined temple of the hawk god Montu at Tod, built under Ptolemy VIII. In such temples Ptolemaic rulers are shown in Egyptian royal dress carrying out the rituals of Egyptian religion.

◁ Terracotta figurine of the Egyptian dwarf god Bes, from Roman Egypt. Bes, the protector of children and pregnant women, was one of the Egyptian deities who became popular with Greek and Roman settlers in Egypt. He holds a Roman shield.

▷ A 2nd-century AD coffin decorated with Egyptian religious scenes and a portrait of the deceased.

Mediterranean Sea

- Mersa Matruh (Paraetonium)
- Gaza
- Rosetta
- Alexandria (Alexandria)
- Tell el-Timai (Thmuis)
- Tell el-Farama (Pelusium)
- (Naukratis)

LOWER EGYPT

- Kom Abu Billo (Terenuthis)
- Tell Atrib (Athribis)

Trajan's Canal

- Saqqara (Memphis)

FAIYUM

- (Arsinoe)
- Ihnasya el-Medina (Herakleopolis)

Siwa Oasis

Bahariya Oasis

- el-Bahnasa (Oxyrhynchus)

Via Hadriana

Eastern Desert

SINAI

- el-Ashmunein (Hermopolis)
- el-Sheikh Ibada (Antinoopolis)
- Tuna el-Gebel (Hermopolis)

UPPER EGYPT

Farafra Oasis

Western Desert

- (Myos Hormos)
- (Mons Porphyrites) PORPHYRY
- (Mons Claudianus) GRANITE
- (Aphrodito)
- Akhmim (Panopolis)
- (Philoteras)

Red Sea

Dakhla Oasis

- Qena (Kaine)
- GOLD
- Quseir (Leukos Limen)
- Dendara (Iunet)
- Qift (Koptos)
- Wadi Hammamat
- Laqeita (Phoinikon)
- Tod
- Luxor (Thebes)
- (Hibis)
- Gebelein (Per-Hathor)
- Esna (Latopolis)
- Edfu (Apollinopolis Magna)

el-Kharga Oasis

- (Mons Smaragdus) EMERALDS
- Kom Ombo (Ombos)

EGYPT NUBIA
- (Philae)
- Aswan (Elephantine)
- Dabod
- LOWER NUBIA (DODEKASCHOINUS)
- (Berenike)
- Kalabsha (Talmis)
- Dendur (Tutzis)
- el-Dakka (Pselchis)

Legend

- Tod — Modern name
- (Talmis) — Ancient name
- Fertile land
- GRANITE — Resource
- ● Site of resource
- ○ Roman way-station
- — Roman road
- --- Desert route
- ■ Capital city
- ● Settlement or site
- Types of site
- ▲ Papyrus
- ◆ Other

Scale 1 : 5 000 000

0 ___ 100km
0 ___ 75miles

Desert finds and Roman roads

Papyrus sites Sites at which papyri or ostraca written on in ancient Greek were found. They include plays and poems, books on medicine and mathematics, and numerous personal letters. Many great works of Greek and Roman literature survive only in copies preserved in the hot dry sand of Egypt. Papyrus production was a major industry in Alexandria.

Roman way-stations The Romans built a road network in the Eastern Desert. Way-stations were provided with water supplies to make it easier for expeditions to cross the desert. The Romans quarried granite and porphyry, a stone used for statues and vessels, and mined for emeralds. The roads led to ports on the Red Sea. The Persian-built canal linking the Nile to the Red Sea was improved under the Emperor Trajan.

△ Egypt in the Greco-Roman Period. In the Ptolemaic era most of the country's wealth was centered on the capital city, Alexandria. Land reclamation schemes and improved irrigation techniques made the Faiyum into a prosperous agricultural area. Many Greeks settled there. They also settled in the oases of the Western Desert which became important again.

Roman rule

Roman Egypt was ruled by Prefects appointed by the Emperor. Temples continued to be built to the Egyptian gods and the worship of Isis spread throughout the Empire. Greek and Roman settlers also adopted some Egyptian burial customs.

The native Egyptians were given little power in their own country. They lived under Roman law and heavy taxation brought poverty to most. Egyptian culture was finally destroyed when Christianity became the official religion of the Roman Empire in the 4th century AD.

WOMEN OF EGYPT

Women were treated better in ancient Egypt than they have been in many other societies. Egyptian women could own and manage property. They had many legal rights and spoke for themselves in court. A woman did not lose control of her own property when she married. If there was a divorce the wife could claim part of her husband's assets to support herself and her children.

Very few women were taught to read and write. This barred them from most careers in government service. Women did serve in temples as part-time priestesses.

Royal women

The women of the royal family were usually priestesses. They played the roles of goddesses in some royal rituals. The mother of the reigning king was an important person.

Royal women could act as regents. Queen Ahhotep ruled on behalf of her young son Ahmose and even led troops into battle. The Great Royal Wife could also be a power in the land. Queen Tiye, the consort of Amonhotep III, was a commoner by birth but foreign kings wrote humble letters to her and she was worshiped as a goddess in her own lifetime.

The throne often passed through the female line and a few women ruled in their own right. Queens like Hatshepsut and Cleopatra VII are among Egypt's most outstanding rulers.

▷ A princess shown standing between the feet of a colossal statue of her father, Ramesses II. She wears an elaborate crown topped by a pair of feathers. Princesses sometimes took on the role of official consort to their fathers.

▽ A group of female entertainers in a banquet scene from an 18th-Dynasty Theban tomb. One woman plays a double flute and another claps out the rhythm while two girls dance naked. The women wear cones of scented fat on top of their wigs. Music, singing and dancing were among the few professions open to women, but such entertainers probably had a low status in society.

▷ The dwarf Seneb embraced by his wife. In front are their young son and daughter. This 6th-Dynasty family group comes from Seneb's tomb at Giza. Later statues often show husbands and wives with their arms around each other.

Family life

The majority of women spent their lives running a household and raising a family. Men were allowed to have more than one wife at a time but very few did.

Egyptian "Wisdom Books," which tell young men how to behave, advise getting married as early as possible. They also warn husbands not to order their wives about at home. Women were competent to run the home without male interference.

The importance of family life is stressed in Egyptian art. Men are regularly shown beside their wives and mothers. Sons and daughters appear making offerings to their parents. Couples hoped for large families but many Egyptian women died young in childbirth.

▷ In this Old Kingdom bedroom scene an important official called Mereruka relaxes while his wife plays the harp. In Egyptian art women are nearly always young, slender and beautiful. Men have skin darkened to reddish-brown by exposure to the sun. Women are given pale yellow skin, suggesting that their place was indoors.

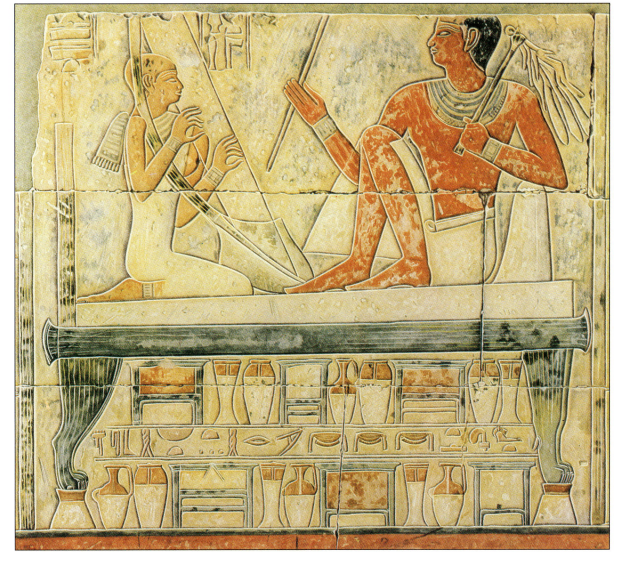

PART TWO

A JOURNEY DOWN THE NILE

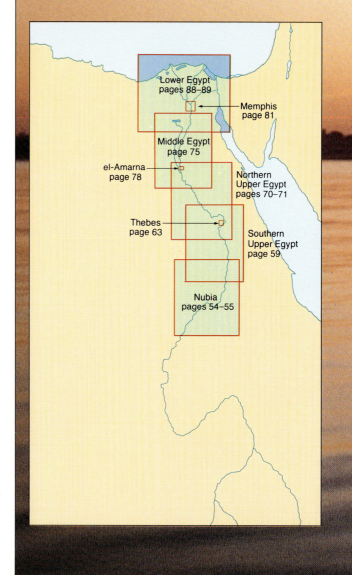

Lower Egypt
pages 88–89

Memphis
page 81

Middle Egypt
page 75

el-Amarna
page 78

Northern
Upper Egypt
pages 70–71

Thebes
page 63

Southern
Upper Egypt
page 59

Nubia
pages 54–55

△ A sphinx from the temple of Ramesses II at el-Sebua, which was flooded with the construction of the Aswan High Dam in the 1960s.

▷ Boats sailing on the Nile. At 4,185mi from its source in Uganda to the tip of the Delta, it is one of the world's longest rivers.

BOATS ON THE NILE

Boats were the most important form of transport in ancient Egypt. The earliest boats were small skiffs made from bundles of papyrus stalks lashed together with ropes. The skiffs were propelled by paddles or long poles. Papyrus skiffs were used throughout Egyptian history for hunting or fishing in the marshes.

At least as early as the Old Kingdom large boats were built in wood. Due to the shortage of tall trees these boats had to be made from numerous small pieces of wood. For seagoing craft and the biggest Nile boats planks of cedar were imported from Lebanon.

In the New Kingdom warships and trading vessels were built in a great dockyard at Memphis. Ships were given names like *The King is Mighty*, *Splendor of the Sun Disc* and *Star in Memphis*.

Sailing the Nile

For most of its course in Upper Egypt the Nile was a broad and placid river. Many branches of the Nile in the Delta were also navigable by large boats. The wind was usually from the north, so sail was used for upstream (southward) journeys. For traveling downstream (north) oars were needed.

The Egyptians never sailed at night. Shifting sandbanks were a major hazard. Sailors kept watch for them from lookout posts. To avoid getting stuck on sandbanks most of the hull of a Nile-going boat had to lie above the waterline. The boats needed to be light, particularly because south of Aswan vessels had to be dragged ashore and hauled past the dangerous cataracts (see map on pages 10-11).

Boats and cargoes

Boats were used for transporting all kinds of cargo from obelisks to cattle. Most Egyptian boats had no keels so their shallow hulls were not very strong. Cargo was usually carried on deck and cabins were also above deck. The heaviest cargoes, such as blocks of Aswan granite, were loaded onto long narrow barges which were towed by other vessels. Most moving of stone was done when the river was at its highest just after the inundation (flood).

Ferries were in constant use for crossing the river. The wealthy had pleasure craft. One story tells that when King Snofru was hot and bored

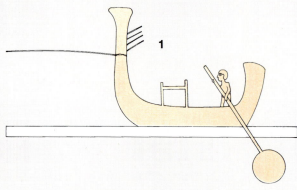

he decided to go for a boat trip rowed by 20 beautiful girls clad only in nets.

The world's oldest boat

The Egyptians imagined the Sun god sailing across the sky in a boat. This may be why full-size boats were included in some Old and Middle Kingdom royal burials. A dismantled boat found in a pit beside the pyramid of Khufu at Giza has been reconstructed and is now in a special museum. The 140ft vessel is made up of 1,224 pieces of cedar. It dates to c. 2528 BC.

In the Middle and New Kingdoms model boats were sometimes put in tombs. Their magical purpose was to help the tomb owner make a pilgrimage to Abydos, the city of Osiris, ruler of the dead. Sacred barques (boats) carried cult statues of gods. On land these statues were often carried in miniature barques by priests.

◁▷ Nile boats of several different dates:
1 *Predynastic* Made from papyrus. It has a tall prow and stern and one large steering oar.
2 *Old Kingdom* Wooden boat with typical Egyptian hull shape. It has steering gear and a double-footed mast. The sail is taller than it is wide.
3 *Middle Kingdom* The steering gear is more elaborate and the mast is collapsible. There is one bank of oars on each side.
4 *Late Period* A boat with a high stern and simple steering gear.

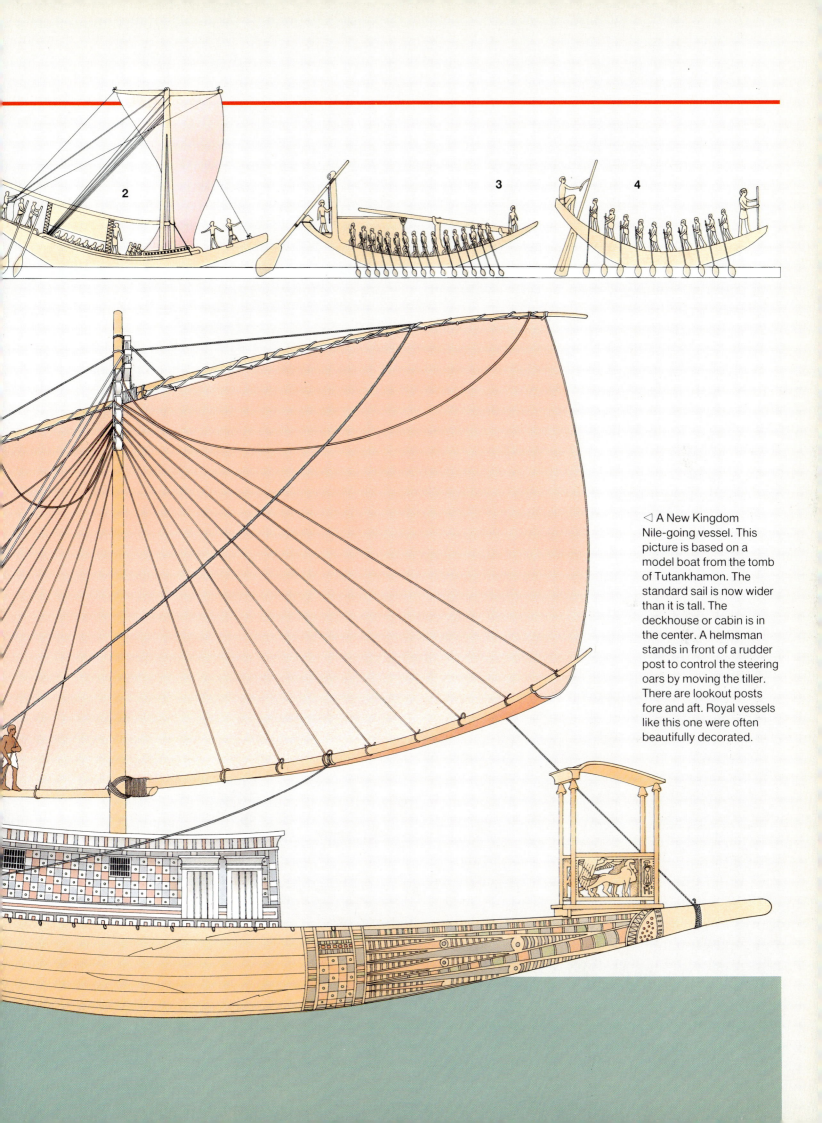

◁ A New Kingdom
Nile-going vessel. This
picture is based on a
model boat from the tomb
of Tutankhamon. The
standard sail is now wider
than it is tall. The
deckhouse or cabin is in
the center. A helmsman
stands in front of a rudder
post to control the steering
oars by moving the tiller.
There are lookout posts
fore and aft. Royal vessels
like this one were often
beautifully decorated.

LOWER NUBIA

In most of ancient Nubia the Nile valley was very narrow. Some Nubian groups settled in the few areas of agricultural land. Others lived as nomads in the deserts. In the Old Kingdom the Egyptians often raided Lower Nubia to capture people and cattle. They also wanted to control the trade routes into Africa and the gold mines of the Nubian desert. In the Middle Kingdom Egypt conquered all of Lower Nubia (see map opposite) and part of Upper Nubia (in present-day Sudan). A series of forts was built along the Nile, mainly in the area of the 2nd and 3rd cataracts. Egypt later lost control of Nubia but some Egyptians continued to live there.

Nubia was reconquered by Egypt in the New Kingdom. Towns and temples were built instead of forts. Perhaps due to years of drought, the population of Lower Nubia was very small by the end of the New Kingdom.

From the Late Period a native dynasty ruled the whole of Nubia. At their capitals of Napata and later Meroe they continued to build temples and pyramids in the Egyptian style for hundreds of years. A few temples to Egyptian and Nubian gods were built in Lower Nubia during the Greco-Roman Period. One Nubian tribe, the Blemmyes, worshiped the goddess Isis long after Egypt had become Christian.

The flooding of Nubia in modern times

The building of the new Aswan "High" Dam in the 1960s meant that much of Lower Nubia was flooded to create a giant reservoir known as Lake Nasser. But the United Nations had by then organized a huge international campaign to dig and record all the main archaeological sites. Many exciting finds were made by archaeologists from all over the world. A great deal was learned about life in ancient Nubia.

The important monuments were moved to safety. Some temples, such as Abu Simbel and Amada, were dismantled and rebuilt on higher ground in the same area. Others, such as Kalabsha, were rebuilt at new sites. A few were reerected outside Egypt. The temple of Dabod now stands in a park in Madrid. A wing was added to the Metropolitan Museum of Art in New York to house the temple of Dendur.

◁ A painting of the temple at Old Kalabsha as it looked in 1839. This was the largest free-standing temple in Lower Nubia. In 1962-63 it was dismantled and some 13,000 blocks of stone were moved to New Kalabsha close to the Aswan High Dam where the temple was rebuilt.

SOUTHERN
UPPER EGYPT
SEE PAGE 59

Aswan (Elephantine)

(Philae)

Aswan High Dam

New Kalabsha

Dabod

Tafa (Taphis)

Beit el-Wali

Old Kalabsha (Talmis)

Dendur (Tutzis)

Gerf Hussein

NUBIA

*Lake
Nasser*

LOWER NUBIA

Wadi Allaqi

New el-Sebua Old el-Sebua

el-Derr Amada

Aniba (Miam)

el-Lessiya

Qasr Ibrim (Primis)

Major town
Other modern town
Location of ancient site
International boundary
Regional boundary
Road
Course of ancient river
Fertile land

Types of ancient site
Settlement
Temple
Tomb

Kor Modern name
(Miam) Ancient name

Abu Simbel

Abahuda

Qustul

EGYPT

SUDAN

Scale 1 : 1 000 000

0   30km

0   20miles

UPPER NUBIA

A   B   C

Abu Simbel: temples

Ramesses II built seven major temples in Nubia. The most famous are the two temples at Abu Simbel. The Great Temple and the Small Temple are built into a sandstone cliff.

Inside are two pillared halls decorated with rock-cut reliefs. Some show the pharaoh in his chariot fighting the Hittites at Qadesh. The boastful Ramesses was very proud of his role in this battle (see also page 64).

The Great Temple was designed so that twice a year the rising sun would reach the innermost part and light up the statues of the gods. In the beautiful Small Temple, the Great Royal Wife Nefertari is shown being crowned as a goddess.

The rescue of the temples

In the 1960s the temples of Abu Simbel were in danger of disappearing beneath Lake Nasser. People from all over the world raised the sum of 40 million dollars to save them. An artificial cliff was built 215ft above the original site. The temples were sawn into large blocks. These were then moved to the new site and put back together again. The work took four and a half years. Now Abu Simbel is a wonder of modern technology as well as a marvel of the ancient world.

1 Terrace
2 Grand entrance with colossi
3 Great pillared hall
4 Side rooms
5 Small pillared hall
6 Anteroom
7 Sanctuary with niche for cult statues

◁ A cutaway view showing the plan of the Great Temple. Most Egyptian temples had a walled forecourt, a grand entrance, one or more pillared (hypostyle) halls and a sanctuary for the cult statues.

Aswan

Abu Simbel

△ A festival of the sun god
at the Great Temple of Abu
Simbel. The most
important festivals were on
the two days of the year
when the sun's rays shone
through the entrance and
along the main axis to
reach the sanctuary.

Here, priests and a high
official arrive by boat for
the festival. In ancient
times statues and reliefs
were often brightly
painted. The temples
would have looked much
more colorful than they do
today.

The rock-cut façade of
the Great Temple has
four 70ft-high statues
of Ramesses II. His
mother, his chief wife
and eight of his 140
children are shown on a
much smaller scale at the
feet of the statues.

SOUTHERN UPPER EGYPT

In ancient times the frontier between Egypt and Nubia was at Biga (see page 60). This island was submerged after the building of the Aswan High Dam. In the first four nomes of Upper Egypt (see page 14), the Nile valley is narrow and the desert is always close. There was not much good agricultural land but the deserts were rich in minerals. Sandstone, granite, diorite, quartzite and steatite (for buildings and statues) were quarried close to Aswan. An amethyst mine was in this area. Gold was mined in the Eastern and Nubian deserts.

A temple from earliest times

The arid climate of Southern Upper Egypt is ideal for preserving ancient remains. We know more about the south than we do about the marshy lands of northern Egypt where excavation is difficult.

The first four nomes of Upper Egypt were important in Predynastic times. Hierakonpolis (modern name Kom el-Ahmar) was one of the earliest towns to be built in Egypt. The Predynastic settlement extended along the edge of the Western Desert.

In the 1st Dynasty a new town and a temple were built on the floodplain. This is the oldest Egyptian temple that we know about in detail. The treasures found in it include mace-heads and palettes that are the only record of some early rulers. There were also ivory figurines, a golden hawk's head and life-size copper statues of two 6th-Dynasty kings.

An ancient town — for the living and the dead

Another site that was important from Predynastic times was Nekheb (modern el-Kab). This developed into a typical Egyptian town. The houses were packed together inside a huge mud-brick enclosure wall. The main temple, dedicated to the local vulture goddess, was inside the town. It was rebuilt many times over a period of nearly 3,000 years. Smaller temples were built on the edge of the desert and the tombs of important people were cut into the desert cliffs.

All main towns had a necropolis, a "city" of the dead with streets of tombs instead of houses. The desert necropolises have often survived when their matching towns on the floodplain have disappeared.

Great temples of the Greco-Roman Period

The most remarkable survival in Southern Upper Egypt is the series of impressive temples dating to Greco-Roman times. There are examples at Philae, Aswan, Kom Ombo, Edfu, el-Kab, Esna and Tod. Though these were built when the country was under foreign rule they are Egyptian in style. Edfu is the most famous but the temples at Esna and Kom Ombo are also outstanding. Esna was dedicated to the ram god Khnum. A calendar inscribed on the walls tells us about the many festivals celebrated here. The temple at Kom Ombo is unusual because the left side is dedicated to one deity and the right side to another.

▽ Part of the Greco-Roman temple overlooking the Nile at Kom Ombo. The chief deities here were Sobek, the crocodile god, and Haroeris – a form of Horus. Sacred crocodiles were reared in a pool in the temple grounds. Mummified sacred crocodiles are preserved in the temple.

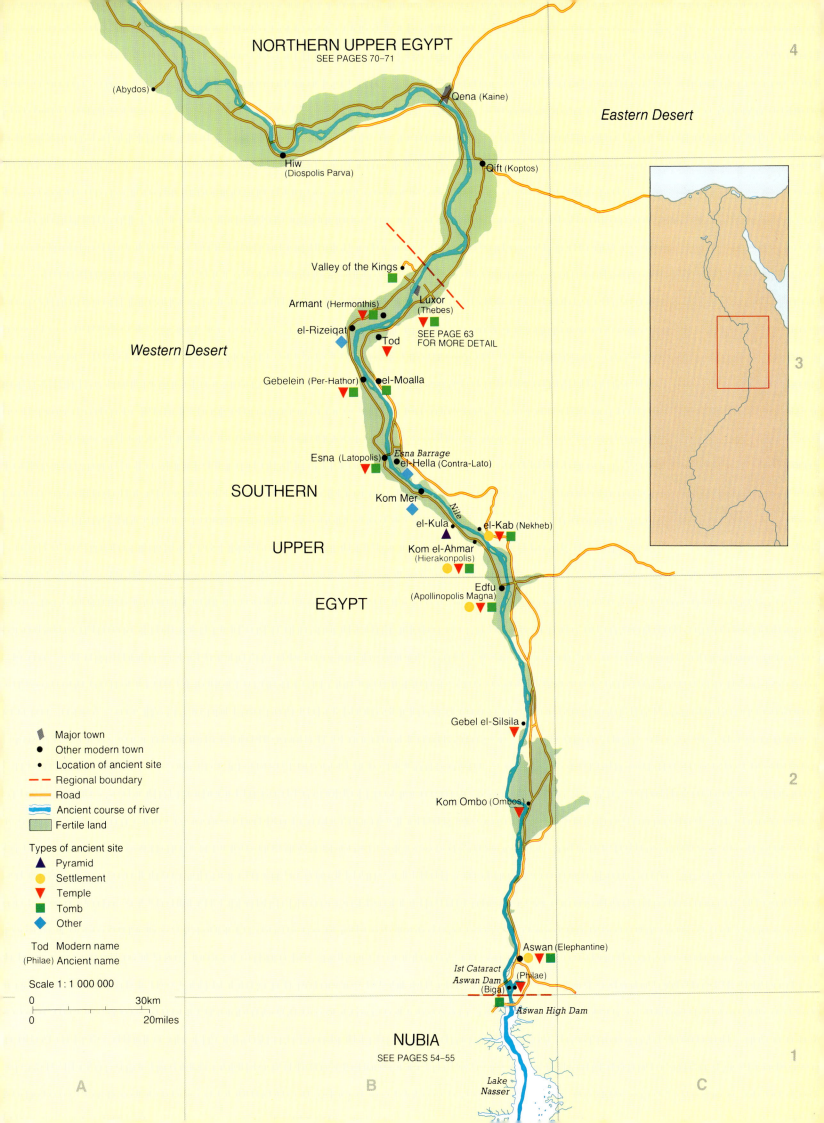

NORTHERN UPPER EGYPT
SEE PAGES 70–71

Eastern Desert

(Abydos) •

Qena (Kaine)

Hiw
(Diospolis Parva)

Qift (Koptos)

Western Desert

Valley of the Kings •

Armant (Hermonthis)

Luxor
(Thebes)

el-Rizeiqat

Tod

SEE PAGE 63
FOR MORE DETAIL

Gebelein (Per-Hathor)

el-Moalla

Esna (Latopolis)

Esna Barrage
el-Hella (Contra-Lato)

SOUTHERN

Kom Mer

Nile

UPPER

el-Kula

el-Kab (Nekheb)

Kom el-Ahmar
(Hierakonpolis)

EGYPT

Edfu
(Apollinopolis Magna)

Gebel el-Silsila •

Kom Ombo (Ombos)

Aswan (Elephantine)

1st Cataract
Aswan Dam
(Philae)
(Biga)

Aswan High Dam

NUBIA
SEE PAGES 54–55

*Lake
Nasser*

Major town
Other modern town
Location of ancient site
Regional boundary
Road
Ancient course of river
Fertile land

Types of ancient site
Pyramid
Settlement
Temple
Tomb
Other

Tod   Modern name
(Philae) Ancient name

Scale 1 : 1 000 000

0   30km
0   20miles

City of Aswan

Aswan took its ancient name of Elephantine from the elephant-ivory trade. The main part of the city was on Elephantine Island in the middle of the Nile. On the east bank of the river were stone quarries and a trading area. Tombs were cut in'the cliffs of the west bank.

Aswan was close to the border between Egypt and Nubia. Troops were stationed there to protect the border and to take part in mining and trading expeditions. All the gold from the Nubian gold mines passed through Aswan. Donkey trains took desert routes from here to trade with African peoples.

In a 6th-Dynasty tomb at Aswan there is an account of some of these trading trips. The tomb owner, a man named Harkhuf, tells how he went south three times. Each trip took seven or eight months. On the third trip he returned home with 300 donkeys carrying precious goods such as ivory, ebony, incense and leopard skins. Best of all he had brought back a pygmy to dance for the king. Harkhuf quotes a letter from King Pepy II. The king, who was only a young boy, was thrilled to hear about the pygmy. He ordered Harkhuf to hurry to the palace by boat. The pygmy was to be guarded day and night. *"Check on him ten times a night!"* wrote Pepy. *"My Majesty wants to see this pygmy more than all the treasures of Sinai and Punt!"*

▽ An unfinished royal statue in the granite quarries east of Aswan. Stone quarried here was used in buildings all over ancient Egypt.

Holy islands – Philae & Biga

Philae and Biga are a pair of islands in the Nile just below Aswan. On Biga was the Abaton, a mound linked with the god Osiris.

When Set murdered Osiris he tore the body into many pieces. Biga was said to be the place where the left leg of Osiris was buried. In one version of the myth Isis, the wife of Osiris, collected the pieces and joined them by magic. Several places claimed to be the site where the whole body of Osiris was buried. Biga was one. The soul of Osiris was thought to haunt the island in the form of a bird. Biga was so holy that only priests could land there.

Philae was sacred to Isis. The temple of Isis was the largest of several temples and shrines on the island. Most of the buildings date to Greco-Roman times. Pilgrims came from all over the Roman Empire to worship Isis here.

The last known inscriptions in ancient Egyptian are at Philae. The religion of Egypt survived on this island for longer than in any other place.

Many of the buildings were in excellent condition until the first Aswan Dam was begun in 1898. After this Philae and Biga were flooded for most of each year. When the second Aswan Dam was constructed they were permanently submerged. The temples of Philae were moved to a nearby island and they are now well above the water level again.

▽ A Roman shrine on Philae island before it was moved to a new site. The discolored stone shows the level reached by the flood waters each year. In the foreground are the remains of the foundations of a small chapel.

Temple at Edfu

There was a walled town at Edfu from the Old Kingdom onwards. The site is now famous for its Temple of Horus. Few buildings from the ancient world are as well preserved as this temple. Inscriptions give many construction details. It was begun under Ptolemy III in 237 BC and took about 180 years to complete.

On the great pylon (gateway) Ptolemy XII strikes a group of prisoners with a mace. Egyptian kings had been shown in this pose for nearly 3,000 years. Inside the temple are reliefs of Horus fighting the enemies of his father Osiris. The evil god Set turns himself into a hippopotamus but Horus hunts him down with a magical harpoon. This story was acted out each year during the festival of *The Coronation of Horus*.

◁ The massive pillars of the hypostyle (Greek for "bearing pillars") hall at Edfu. The hall imitates a thicket of marsh plants. On some pillars the figures of the gods were damaged by early Christians and have been almost erased.

▽ The modern town of Edfu is dominated by the great temple dedicated to the god Horus. Its wonderful state of preservation is clear from this aerial view. The mound beyond the temple is the site of the ancient town.

THE GREAT CITY OF THEBES

In the time of the Old Kingdom Thebes was just a provincial town. When a local dynasty reunited Egypt after the First Intermediate Period Thebes became an important administrative and religious center. From the New Kingdom onwards it was one of the largest urban areas in Egypt. Its magnificent buildings were famous throughout the ancient world. Thebes is a Greek name. The Egyptians called the city "Waset."

The total area of Thebes was about 3 sq.mi. The city spread on both sides of the Nile. The east bank was for the living and the west bank mainly for the dead. The site of Eastern Thebes is largely covered by the modern town of Luxor. Little remains of the ancient houses and palaces but some of the great stone temples do survive.

The city of the dead — a giant cemetery
Western Thebes was dominated by the mountain known as "the Peak." The Egyptians believed that this mountain was an entrance to the underworld. Many tombs were cut into the cliffs and ravines close to the Peak. This necropolis was called "The Place of Truth."

Many people lived and worked in the necropolis. The craftsmen's village at Deir el-Medina is very well preserved. We know more about these craftsmen than about any other ancient Egyptian community.

The valley of the kings
The pyramid burials of Old and Middle Kingdom rulers were soon robbed of their treasures. From the 18th Dynasty a new plan was tried. Enene, the chief architect of Amonhotep I and Thutmose I, tells us that *"I oversaw the cutting out of the rock-tomb of his Majesty in a lonely place where nobody could look on."* This lonely place was the Valley of the Kings.

Throughout the New Kingdom rulers were buried in tombs hidden in this valley. Mortuary temples were built on the west bank to serve the cult of the dead kings. Some rulers also built palaces in Western Thebes. The largest was the palace of Amonhotep III at Malqata.

▽ A painted burial chamber in the Theban city of the dead (necropolis). This is the tomb of Pashed. He was one of the artists who worked on the royal tombs. The entrance to the burial chamber is flanked by the jackal god Anubis, who guarded the dead. On the rear wall are the gods who judge the dead.

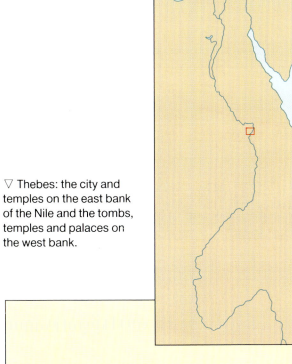

▽ Thebes: the city and temples on the east bank of the Nile and the tombs, temples and palaces on the west bank.

▷ The west bank of the Nile at Thebes. Kings built temples along the edge of the floodplain and against these cliffs. The royal tombs are in the hills behind.

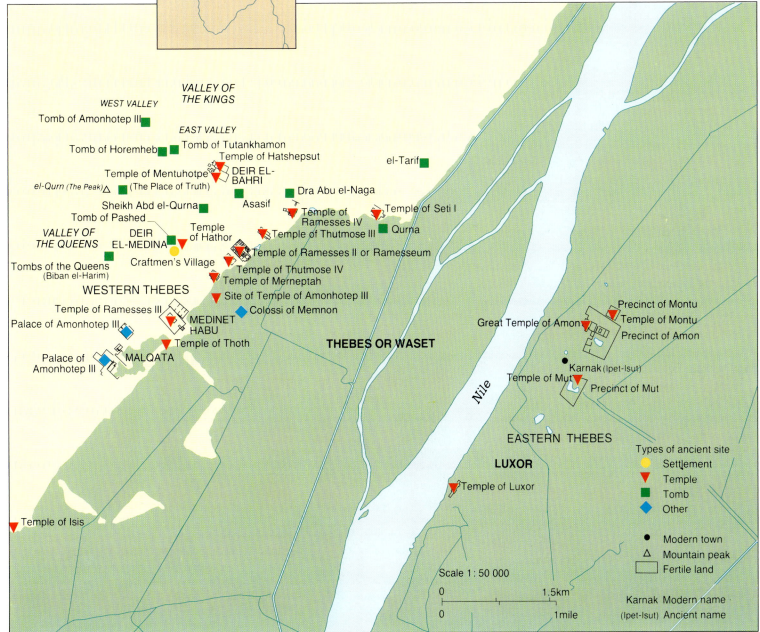

VALLEY OF THE KINGS

WEST VALLEY

Tomb of Amonhotep III

EAST VALLEY

Tomb of Horemheb   Tomb of Tutankhamon
                    Temple of Hatshepsut   el-Tarif

Temple of Mentuhotpe   DEIR EL-
el-Qurn (The Peak)△   (The Place of Truth)   BAHRI

                        Dra Abu el-Naga

Sheikh Abd el-Qurna   Asasif   Temple of Seti I
Tomb of Pashed   Temple of
                                      Ramesses IV
VALLEY OF   DEIR   Qurna
THE QUEENS   EL-MEDINA   Temple   Temple of Thutmose III
             of Hathor

Tombs of the Queens   Craftmen's Village   Temple of Ramesses II or Ramesseum
(Biban el-Harim)
                        Temple of Thutmose IV
WESTERN THEBES   Temple of Merneptah

Temple of Ramesses III   Site of Temple of Amonhotep III

Palace of Amonhotep III   Colossi of Memnon   THEBES OR WASET
                MEDINET
                HABU   Precinct of Montu
                        Temple of Thoth   Temple of Montu
Palace of   Great Temple of Amon
Amonhotep III   MALQATA   Precinct of Amon

                                          Karnak (Ipet-Isut)
                                Temple of Mut
                                                Precinct of Mut

                                          Nile

                                    EASTERN THEBES

                                    LUXOR

Types of ancient site

● Settlement (yellow)
▽ Temple (red)
■ Tomb (green)
◆ Other (blue)

                    Temple of Luxor

Temple of Isis

● Modern town
△ Mountain peak
▢ Fertile land

Scale 1 : 50 000

0   1.5km

0   1mile

Karnak   Modern name
(Ipet-Isut) Ancient name

Pylon, pillars & obelisks at Luxor

The god Amon had two main temples in Thebes: Karnak in the north of the city and Luxor in the south. Most of the Luxor temple was built in the 18th Dynasty during the reign of Amonhotep III. A courtyard and pylon (gateway) were added by Ramesses II. An avenue of sphinxes joining Luxor to Karnak was set up in the Late Period.

Luxor has one of the most impressive entrances of any Egyptian temple. The pylon is decorated with the favorite subject of Ramesses II: his own bravery at the battle of Qadesh (see page 56). Outside the pylon are several colossal statues of this pharaoh. A pair of red granite obelisks once stood here but one of them was taken to Paris in 1833.

The great procession of the Festival of Opet
The temple has two courtyards. They are linked by a narrow colonnade, which formed a route for processions. The walls of this processional way are decorated with scenes from the Festival of Opet. At this annual festival the Amon of Karnak visited Luxor for 11 days.

The cult statues of Amon, his wife Mut and their son Khons, were placed in magnificently decorated barques. Huge crowds gathered on the east bank of the Nile to watch the barques towed from Karnak to Luxor. On shore the procession included musicians, dancers and acrobats. Questions might be put to the god at this time. Occasionally the heir to the throne seems to have been chosen by Amon during the Festival of Opet.

Deep inside the temple is a room decorated with reliefs telling the story of the birth of Amonhotep III. They show Amon taking the form of King Thutmose IV to visit Queen Mutemwiya. Many goddesses come to nurse and protect the queen's son. The young prince is then brought before his father Amon and the gods decide to give him a long reign.

Close to this room is an area of the temple that was turned into a shrine to the Roman emperors around AD 300. Nearly a thousand years later a mosque was built in the courtyard of Ramesses II. This is still in use.

▷ A view of Luxor from the southwest. The mosque (Muslim place of worship) built into the temple can be seen on the right.

▽ The pylon and courtyard built by Ramesses II. Behind are the tall columns of the processional way.

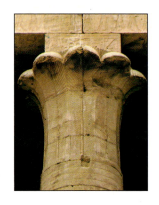
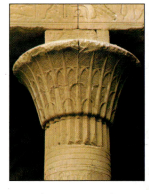
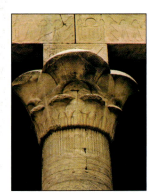

△ Most Egyptian columns are based on plant life. These three capitals (column tops) are from Edfu. Left: Capital in the form of a crown of palm fronds. Center: Papyriform columns have capitals in the shape of papyrus flower-heads (umbels). They can be shown open (above) or as a closed bud. Right: An elaborate capital decorated with a group of papyrus umbels.

Temple complex at Karnak

Karnak is the site of a group of temples covering an area of about 1 sq. mi. The most important was the Great Temple of Amon. The name Amon means "the hidden one" and he was the god of invisible forces such as wind. He was not an important deity until the Middle Kingdom. Very little of the Middle Kingdom temple survives. Every Egyptian ruler wanted to please Amon by putting up splendid buildings for him at Karnak. This often meant knocking down the old buildings and reusing their stones. The Great Temple was continually enlarged and rebuilt over a period of 2,000 years.

The Triumph of Amon

In the early 18th Dynasty Thebes became the capital of Egypt. Amon's name was linked with that of the sun god Ra. This new deity Amon-Ra was credited with the creation of the world.

During the New Kingdom Karnak became the largest and wealthiest temple complex in Egypt. The Great Temple of Amon was once surrounded by tall mud-brick walls. This enclosed area includes a sacred lake and many lesser temples and shrines. The eastern part of the Great Temple complex is the oldest. Kings kept on building new entrances so the temple now has ten massive pylons (gateways).

Between the second and third pylons is the Great Hypostyle Hall, the most famous part of the temple. The hall was begun by Seti I and finished by Ramesses II. The roof of this vast hall is supported by 134 elaborate columns. The 12 columns in the central aisle are each 72ft high. Behind four more pylons lies the sanctuary area. Another series of pylons and courtyards joins on from the south. In one courtyard 751 stone statues and stelae and 17,000 bronze figurines were found buried.

The other main buildings at Karnak include a temple to the Theban god Montu. Separate temples were built for Mut, the consort of Amon, and for their son Khons. The temple of Mut once held over 600 black granite statues of the lioness goddess Sekhmet.

△ An avenue of sphinxes linked Karnak to a canal. Each statue shows Amon as a ram-headed lion with a king standing between his front paws.

▽ This beautiful chapel at Karnak is a rare survivor from the Middle Kingdom. The pillars and intricate reliefs were recovered in pieces from inside a New Kingdom pylon (gateway).

Temples & tombs of the City of the Dead

After king Mentuhotpe reunited Egypt in 2040 BC he built himself a tomb and temple on the west bank at Deir el-Bahri. Nearly 600 years later Queen Hatshepsut built her beautiful temple against the dramatic cliffs of Deir el-Bahri. Thutmose III also built here but his temple has been badly damaged by repeated rock falls.

Later kings built closer to the edge of the floodplain. Only two huge statues known as the Colossi of Memnon remain at the mortuary temple of Amonhotep III. The temple of Ramesses II is called the Ramesseum. In 1165 BC necropolis workmen demonstrated outside this temple in a dispute over wages. This is the earliest known strike. A whole town grew up around the great temple of Ramesses III at Medinet Habu. The king was nearly the victim of a murder plot while staying in a palace next to this temple.

▷ Two men pick grapes in a vine arbor – one of the many vivid scenes from daily life painted on the walls of 18th-Dynasty Theban tombs. The men would then crush the grapes by treading on them in a vat and use the liquid to make wine.

▷ The "Colossi of Memnon" are statues of Amonhotep III. They are nearly 60ft high. After the northern statue was damaged in an earthquake in 27BC, it made a strange sound at dawn. This "singing" stopped when the statue was repaired in the 3rd century AD.

• Valley of the Kings
• Deir el-Bahri
• Valley of the Queens
• Medinet Habu

• Luxor
  (Thebes)

▷ Funeral scenes are also common in Theban tombs. Here a mummy fitted with a mask is carried by four men. A fifth man burns incense in an arm-shaped holder.

Tombs in the city of the dead (necropolis)

All kinds of people were buried in the Theban necropolis. One 11th-Dynasty tomb held the bodies of 60 soldiers killed in battle. New Kingdom craftsmen took time off from royal projects to decorate their own tombs. The so-called Tombs of the Nobles are those of high officials. Many New Kingdom examples contain wonderful paintings or reliefs. Some of these tombs are unfinished because their owners suddenly fell from royal favor.

Members of the royal family were buried in the Valley of the Queens. The finest tomb there belongs to Queen Nefertari. Its paintings are now badly damaged by rock salt.

The royal mummies

In the Valley of the Kings 62 tombs have been found. In each one, rock-cut passages and stairways lead down past one or more halls to the burial chamber. The walls are decorated with religious scenes. The most elaborate tombs are those of Seti I and Ramesses VI.

Each king was buried with a fortune in funerary goods. By the end of the New Kingdom most of the tombs in the valley had been robbed. Under the 21st Dynasty many of the royal mummies were moved to a secret hiding place and they lay undiscovered until 1881. The great New Kingdom rulers now rest in the Egyptian Museum, Cairo.

▷ A painted relief in the tomb of Horemheb in the Valley of the Kings. This tomb was designed to foil thieves. The first room was made to look like a dead-end by concealing the door to the next room behind a solid-looking decorated wall. In the second room the stairway to the burial chamber was hidden under the floor. In spite of these tricks, the tomb was soon robbed of its treasure.

THE TREASURES OF TUTANKHAMON

The most famous tomb in the Valley of the Kings is that of Tutankhamon. Little is known about this short-lived ruler. He was probably the son of Akhenaten by a lesser wife called Kiya. As a boy his name was Tutankhaten. The throne passed to Tutankhaten in c. 1333 BC when he was about seven years old. The boy king was married to one of the six daughters of Akhenaten and his chief wife Nefertiti.

After a few years at el-Amarna the court returned to Thebes and Memphis. Akhenaten's new capital and religion were both abandoned. Amon became the chief god of Egypt again and the king changed his name from Tutankhaten to Tutankhamon. Only ten years after he came to the throne Tutankhamon died. The cause of death may have been a head injury.

A hasty burial

Due to the king's early death, his tomb in the Valley of the Kings was not ready. A small tomb that had probably been cut for the vizier Aya was hastily decorated for a royal burial. A huge quantity of precious objects was crammed into its four rooms.

Shortly after the burial two attempts were made to rob the tomb. The fingerprints of one of the thieves are still visible inside an ointment jar. Necropolis guards discovered the crimes before much was taken. The tomb was quickly tidied up and resealed. Its entrance was probably soon hidden by landslips. Rubble from building work on the nearby tomb of Ramesses VI buried the entrance still deeper.

The discovery of the tomb

In 1917 an English Egyptologist named Howard Carter began excavating in the Valley of the Kings. No unrobbed royal burial had ever been found in the valley but Tutankhamon's tomb was still unlocated. With financial support from his patron, Lord Carnarvon, Carter spent six digging seasons searching for the tomb. He almost gave up but in November 1922 a rock-cut step was found. A stairway leading down to a sealed entrance was quickly uncovered. Lord Carnarvon hurried out to Egypt for the opening of the tomb. The doorway had the unbroken seals of ancient necropolis guards.

The first discovery was an antechamber crowded with marvelous objects. There were

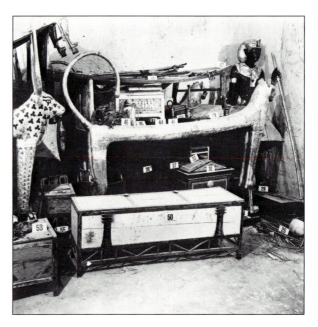

▷ A tender scene adorning part of the golden throne of Tutankhamon. The young king is shown in a relaxed pose. His wife, Queen Ankhesenamon, rubs scented oil into his jeweled collar.

The throne is made from gold-plated wood decorated with silver and gold leaf, semiprecious stones and glass.

◁ This photograph, taken shortly after the opening of Tutankhamon's tomb, reveals part of the antechamber. It shows how the treasures were piled together to fit into a small space. The life-size statue in the corner is of Tutankhamon.

▽ The funeral procession of Tutankhamon. The royal coffins, weighing over 2,900lb, lie on a movable frame inside a barque (boat) shrine. The shrine, mounted on a sledge, is dragged along by courtiers and a team of oxen. The courtiers wear white headbands, a sign of mourning. Next comes an alabaster shrine shouldered by priests. This holds the four canopic jars containing the liver, lungs, stomach and intestines of Tutankhamon.

statues and chariots and animal-shaped funerary beds. The furniture included thrones, stools, chests and painted boxes. Among the smaller items were alabaster vases, golden jewelry, gloves, sandals, riding crops, bronze trumpets and ostrich-feather fans.

The golden treasures

The burial chamber was filled by four gilded shrines. Inside the innermost shrine was the red sandstone sarcophagus of Tutankhamon. The mummy was protected by a set of three coffins. Between the coffins were the dried remains of garlands of olive and willow leaves and lotus flowers. Carter was amazed to find that the third coffin was made from nearly 2,500lb of pure gold. Inside this coffin was the mummy itself, its head covered in a beautiful golden portrait mask.

The body of Tutankhamon was in bad condition as too many precious ointments had been used on it. The king's vital organs were in an alabaster chest in another room. It took about ten years of careful work to clear the tomb of all its treasures. Most of the objects are on display in the Egyptian Museum, Cairo.

NORTHERN UPPER EGYPT

Northern Upper Egypt was the heartland of ancient Egypt. The Badarian and Naqada cultures, from which Egyptian civilization developed, are named after sites in this area. The presence of gold in the Eastern Desert was a vital factor in the rise of an early kingdom centered on Northern Upper Egypt. Just as important were trade routes from this area to the Red Sea, particularly the Wadi Hammamat.

Three important early towns, Ombos, Qus and Koptos were all close to this Wadi (set along the road from Qift). Gold mines and stone quarries lay here. Dismantled ships were carried through the Wadi on the 100mi journey to the Red Sea coast. When the coast was reached the ships were put together. They then sailed north to carry turquoise mining expeditions to Sinai or south to Punt (Somalia) or the Yemen to fetch spices and incense.

A holy place

Another site that began to be important in early times was Abydos. Some Predynastic kings and most 1st- and 2nd-Dynasty rulers had tombs close to Abydos at Umm el-Qaab. Abydos was a religious rather than a political center. Its main god was Khentamentiu ("Chief of the Westerners"). The Westerners were the spirits of the dead who had reached the Egyptian paradise – "The Beautiful West." From the late Old Kingdom, Khentamentiu was identified with the god Osiris.

In the Middle and New Kingdoms Abydos was the most important of the places that claimed to be the burial place of Osiris. Every year the story of how Osiris was murdered and brought back to life was acted out. This festival attracted pilgrims from all over the country. Every Egyptian hoped to visit Abydos at least once in a lifetime.

It was thought that anyone who had a tomb or a monument at Abydos would share in the resurrection of Osiris. Some kings built mortuary temples where offerings were made to their spirits. Ordinary people put up stelae or cenotaphs so that their spirits could join with Osiris in his triumph over death.

The shadow of Thebes

From the Middle Kingdom onwards the growth of Thebes overshadowed all the other towns in Northern Upper Egypt. New Kingdom rulers did build temples at Abydos, Koptos and Dendara but the temples of Thebes were larger and richer. Thebes stayed the most important political and religious center in the area until the end of the Late Period.

Under Greek and Roman rule other towns flourished. Northern Upper Egypt has a fine series of temples dating to the Greco-Roman Period. They can be found at Nag el-Madamud, Qus, Dendara, Hiw, Akhmim and Wannina. These temples usually replaced earlier buildings. The most outstanding is the temple of Hathor at Dendara. This was the last great example of Egyptian architecture to be built.

▷ A scene from the royal chapel in the temple built by Seti I at Abydos. This relief has most of its original paintwork. The dead and mummified king is shown seated on a throne being honored as a god.

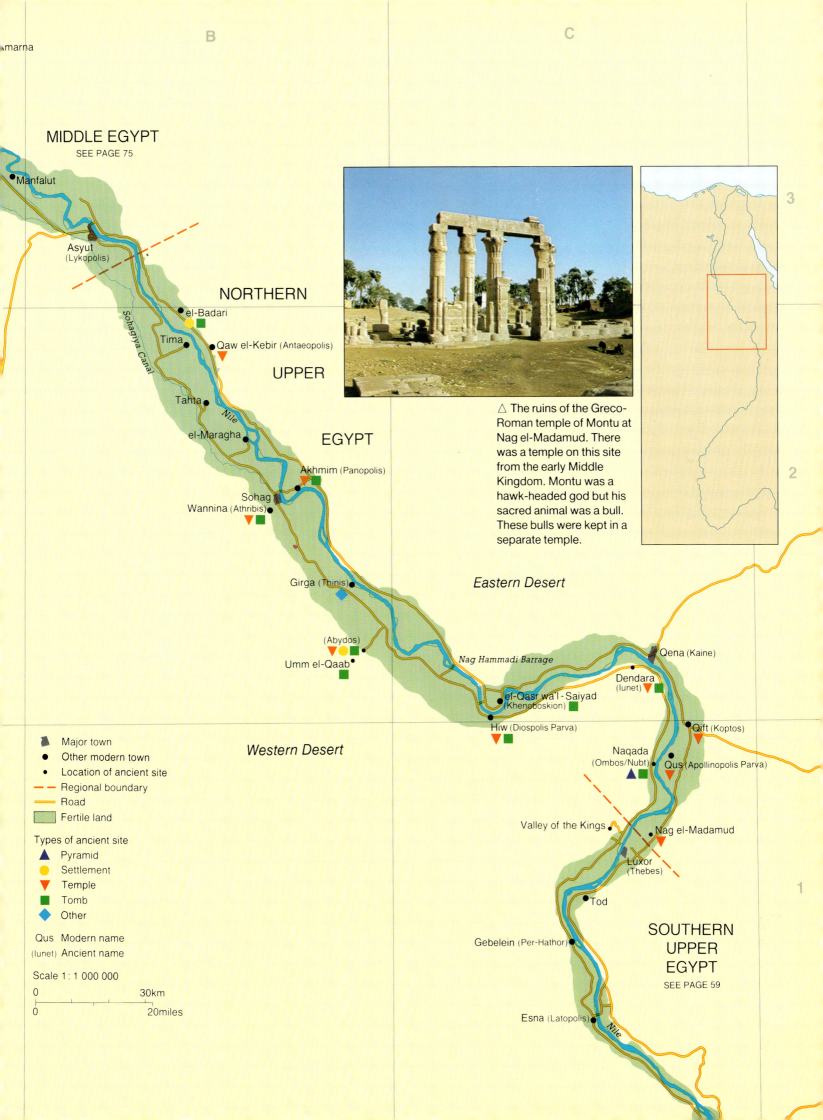

..marna

MIDDLE EGYPT
SEE PAGE 75

Manfalut

Asyut
(Lykopolis)

NORTHERN

el-Badari

Tima

Qaw el-Kebir (Antaeopolis)

UPPER

Tahta

Nile

el-Maragha

EGYPT

Akhmim (Panopolis)

Sohag

Wannina (Athribis)

Sohagiya Canal

Girga (Thinis)

(Abydos)

Umm el-Qaab

Eastern Desert

△ The ruins of the Greco-
Roman temple of Montu at
Nag el-Madamud. There
was a temple on this site
from the early Middle
Kingdom. Montu was a
hawk-headed god but his
sacred animal was a bull.
These bulls were kept in a
separate temple.

Nag Hammadi Barrage

Qena (Kaine)

Dendara
(Iunet)

el-Qasr wa'l-Saiyad
(Khenoboskion)

Qift (Koptos)

Hiw (Diospolis Parva)

Naqada
(Ombos/Nubt)

Qus (Apollinopolis Parva)

Western Desert

Valley of the Kings

Nag el-Madamud

Luxor
(Thebes)

Tod

SOUTHERN
UPPER
EGYPT

SEE PAGE 59

Gebelein (Per-Hathor)

Esna (Latopolis)

Nile

2

1

Legend:

■ Major town
● Other modern town
• Location of ancient site
– – – Regional boundary
—— Road
▨ Fertile land

Types of ancient site
▲ Pyramid
● Settlement
▼ Temple
■ Tomb
◆ Other

Qus   Modern name
(Iunet)   Ancient name

Scale 1 : 1 000 000

0   30km

0   20miles

Shrines at Dendara

Dendara was an important town in the Old Kingdom and the First Intermediate Period. Tombs from this era survive on the desert edge. Dendara was the main cult center of Hathor. She was a goddess of birth and death. She was also linked with love, music, foreign lands and precious minerals.

Every year the cult statue of Hathor made the journey from Dendara to Edfu for the festival of her "marriage" to Horus. Hathor, Horus and their son Ihy each had their own temple at Dendara. Only the temple complex of Hathor still stands.

The sacred area

Inside the enclosure wall of the Hathor temple is a sacred lake. Priests washed in such lakes to make themselves pure before entering a sanctuary. Among the buildings surrounding the Hathor temple are a sanatorium and two "birth houses." Sick people slept in the sanatorium. They hoped that Hathor would tell them in a dream how they could be cured. Patients also drank or bathed in sacred water.

A "birth house" is a shrine celebrating the birth of a deity. At Dendara reliefs in the two "birth houses" show Hathor giving birth to her son. Women prayed to Hathor, Lady of Dendara, to bring them safely through the ordeal of childbirth.

The temple of Hathor

The temple of Hathor was built and decorated between the 2nd century BC and the 1st century AD. It has two splendid columned halls. Several shrines were built on top of the temple's flat roof. Sacred treasures were once hidden in small underground rooms near the sanctuary. On the rear wall of the temple Cleopatra VII appears with her son by Julius Caesar (see page 46). In the middle of this wall is a huge symbol of Hathor. Most visitors prayed to the goddess at this spot.

▷ The outer columned hall at Dendara. Four faces of the goddess Hathor form the capital to each column. When decorating halls like these the artists used wooden scaffolding and worked from the top down.

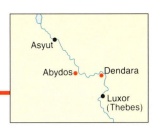

Temples & tombs at Abydos

Little survives of the ancient town of Abydos or of the main temple of Osiris that was inside the town walls. The great necropolis of Abydos spreads for about 1mi along the edge of the Western Desert. Burials were made here for over three thousand years.

The Mother of Pots

The early royal tombs at Umm el-Qaab had brick-lined underground burial chambers. Some 1st Dynasty kings also built large mud-brick enclosures close to the town. These may have been used to store grave goods. The tomb of King Djer was later thought to be the burial place of Osiris. Umm el-Qaab means "The Mother of Pots." It gets its name from the thousands of pottery fragments left by pilgrims to the tomb of Osiris. Stone slabs (stelae) and monuments (cenotaphs) were set up along the route from this tomb to the main temple of Osiris.

The Temple of Seti I

Several kings built mortuary temples in the southern part of Abydos. By far the best preserved is the temple of King Seti I. This is built in fine white limestone. There were originally two pylons, two courtyards and two columned halls. The plan of the inner area is unique. It has seven sanctuaries side by side. The reliefs in these sanctuaries are among the most delicate and beautiful in all Egyptian art.

One sanctuary was for the cult of Seti himself. Another is dedicated to Osiris. A group of rooms for the worship of Osiris, Isis and Horus opens off this sanctuary. Scenes from the myth of Osiris decorate the walls. In another part of the temple Seti is shown with his heir Ramesses II making offerings to a list of royal ancestors. Ramesses completed his father's temple and built his own nearby.

Behind the temple of Seti I is a mysterious building known as the Osireion. It was probably begun under Seti I and finished by his grandson Merneptah. The main feature was an underground hall built in red granite. An artificial island was constructed in the middle of the hall and a canal dug to surround the island with water. A sarcophagus was placed on the island. This building could be a dummy royal tomb, a model of the tomb of Osiris or a re-creation of the first mound of land rising above the waters of chaos.

▽ A painted relief from the temple of Ramesses II at Abydos. Animals such as fattened oxen are led in to be sacrificed to the gods. Major temples had their own slaughter-houses. After the joints of meat had been offered to the gods, they were shared out among the priests as part of their wages. At a festival, more than a 100 animals might be killed in a day to feed the visiting crowds.

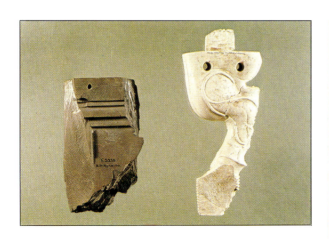

△ Furniture fragments from royal tombs at Abydos. They are nearly 5,000 years old. Left: A piece of carved stone. Right: An ivory bed leg in the form of a bull's leg. Egyptian beds usually had a wooden frame covered by rush-matting. On top of this went a mattress and linen sheets.

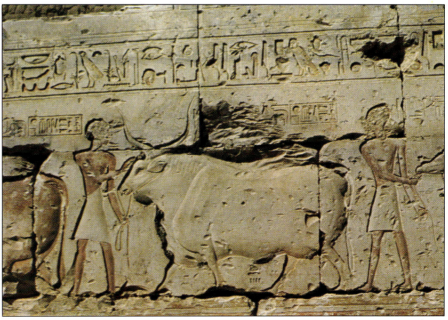

MIDDLE EGYPT

The term Middle Egypt describes some 180mi of the Nile valley from Asyut to Memphis. It also includes the Faiyum, a large area of fertile land jutting out into the Western Desert. A branch of the Nile flowed through the Faiyum into Lake Moeris. This lake was much larger in ancient times than it is today.

Royal tombs and cities

Middle Egypt has few large temples but it does have many interesting tombs. Some kings were buried in this area. There is a 3rd/4th-Dynasty royal pyramid at Maidum and Middle Kingdom rulers built pyramids at el-Lisht, el-Lahun and Hawara.

These 12th-Dynasty pyramids were poorly constructed and are now in ruins. The vast mortuary temple of Amenemhet III at Hawara was famous in the ancient world as "The Labyrinth." Almost nothing of it survives. Nor has any trace been found of the 12th-Dynasty capital Itjtawy, which lay somewhere near el-Lisht. In the 18th Dynasty another capital city and royal necropolis was built in Middle Egypt at el-Amarna.

The nomarchs of Middle Egypt

From the 6th Dynasty to the late 12th Dynasty the nomarchs of Middle Egypt enjoyed much power and independence. They built splendid rock-cut tombs and were buried in coffins

painted with maps of the underworld. The nomarchs of Herakleopolis called themselves kings in the First Intermediate Period. Both Herakleopolis and Hermopolis were the capital towns of some minor kings during the Third Intermediate Period.

Hermopolis was the main cult center of the god Thoth. A huge temple complex once stood here. Among the surviving monuments are two colossal statues of Thoth as a baboon. Sacred baboons and ibises, the bird of Thoth, were buried in underground galleries in the necropolis at Tuna el-Gebel. This necropolis has painted tombs of the Greco-Roman Period.

△ A blue faience hippopotamus from a tomb at Meir. The body is decorated with marsh plants. This charming figurine dates to the late 20th century BC. Model animals have been found in many Middle Kingdom tombs.

◁ A Middle Kingdom temple at Qasr el-Sagha in the desert north of the Faiyum. In ancient times part of Lake Moeris reached almost to this site. Most of the monuments in the Faiyum area date to the Middle Kingdom or the Greco-Roman Period. Crocodiles were once common in Lake Moeris. When Egyptians had to cross water they chanted spells against being snatched by a crocodile.

SEE ALSO
PAGES 88–89

• Qasr el-Sagha

el-Lisht (Itjtawy)

*Birket Qarun
(Lake Moeris)*

Maidum

Atfih
(Aphroditopolis)

Medinet el-Faiyum (Krokodilopolis)

Seila

FAIYUM

Hawara

el-Wasta

el-Lahun

Kom Medinet Ghurab

Sidmant el-Gebel

Ihnasya el-Medina (Herakleopolis)

Beni Suef

Western Desert

el-Fashn

el-Hiba (Ankyronon Polis)

Bahr Yusuf

MIDDLE   **EGYPT**

el-Bahnasa (Oxyrhynchus)

Beni Mazar

Samalut

Tihna (Akoris)

el-Minya (Menat-Khufu)

Zawyet el-Amwat

Beni Hasan

(Speos Artemidos)

el-Ashmunein (Hermopolis)

Tuna el-Gebel (Hermopolis)

Deir el-Bersha

Mallawi

el-Sheikh Said

el-Amarna (Akhetaten)

SEE PAGE 78
FOR MORE DETAIL

Dairut

Meir (Cusae)

el-Qusiya (Cusae)

Deir el-Gabrawi

Manfalut

Abnub

Sohagiya Canal

Nile

Asyut

Asyut
(Lykopolis)

**NORTHERN
UPPER EGYPT**
SEE PAGES 70–71

Major town

Other modern town

Location of ancient site

Regional boundary

Road

Fertile land

Types of ancient site

▲ Pyramid

● Settlement

▼ Temple

■ Tomb

◆ Other

Meir   Modern name

(Cusae) Ancient name

Scale 1 : 1 000 000

0   30km

0   20miles

Nile

3

2

1

A   B

Rock tombs at Meir

Meir is the site of the necropolis for the ancient town of Cusae. This town, of which nothing survives, was the administrative center of a nome. The rock-cut tombs at Meir belong to nomarchs of the 6th and 12th Dynasties.

Each tomb consists of a large room cut inside the cliff-face. There are niches for statues and offerings and deep shafts for the coffins. The walls are decorated with painted reliefs. Hunting in the desert and fishing in the marshes are common scenes.

A festival of Hathor is illustrated in several of the tombs. The late 12th-Dynasty tomb of Wekh-hotep has some of the most delicate paintings to survive from the Middle Kingdom. This nomarch is shown spearing fish and throwing a boomerang at marsh birds.

▽ A family group from a late 12th-Dynasty tomb at Meir. The nomarch (local ruler) Wekh-hotep is shown with his two wives and a small daughter.

Collapsed pyramid at Maidum

Maidum is the site of a mysterious building disaster. A curious tower rising from a mound of rubble is all that remains of an early attempt to build a true pyramid. This pyramid was probably begun for Huni, the last king of the 3rd Dynasty, and completed by his successor Snofru.

The Maidum pyramid started as a seven-stepped structure. Then an eighth step was built. Finally the steps were filled in and a limestone casing was added to create a smooth-sided pyramid. This outer casing was not well laid and it had no proper foundations. As a result the pyramid collapsed. It is not clear whether this happened just after the pyramid was finished or hundreds of years later. Close to the pyramid are some early 4th-Dynasty mastaba (flat-roofed) tombs.

▽ A view of the tower-shaped core of the collapsed pyramid at Maidum. It stands on a "hill" formed by stone debris. A causeway runs up to a small temple on the east side of the pyramid. This was where offerings were made to the dead king.

△ The rubble core of the Maidum pyramid is now visible in places. When the foundations collapsed the outer walls slid down to form a tower shape.

▽ A section of the Maidum pyramid showing its three stages:
1 Seven-stepped pyramid.
2 Eight-stepped pyramid.
3 True geometric pyramid.

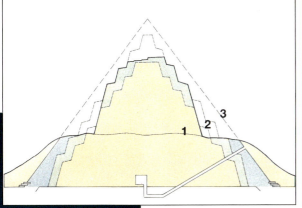

Painted rooms at Beni Hasan

Decorated rock-cut tombs belonging to Middle Egyptian nomarchs survive at Asyut, Deir el-Gabrawi, Meir, el-Sheikh Said, Deir el-Bersha and Beni Hasan. The most interesting are the group at Beni Hasan. There are 39 tombs here dating from the 11th to the late 12th Dynasties. Wooden coffins, statuettes and models have been found in them. The more elaborate tombs have an outer court and portico and a rock-cut main room with elegant pillars. The decoration is painted, not carved.

The ceilings are painted with geometric patterns to imitate matting or textiles. Scenes from daily life cover most of the wall space. Unusual paintings of battles and sieges illustrate wars between nomes. Gentler scenes include girls playing ball, men and baboons harvesting figs and the arrival of a group of traders from Palestine. The paintings have recently been restored.

In a nearby valley Queen Hatshepsut built a small temple. This unfinished rock-cut temple is known as Speos Artemidos. It was dedicated to a lioness goddess called Pakhet. Her name means "she who scratches."

▽ A model boat made from wood and linen. It comes from a 12th-Dynasty tomb at Beni Hasan. A mummy is shown on deck on a bier (a funerary bed) under a canopy. The dead person is being taken to Abydos to share in the death and rebirth of Osiris. The model boat was thought to make this journey by magic. There was then no need for the real mummy to be taken to Abydos. Model boats have been found in many rock-cut tombs in Middle Egypt.

City of el-Amarna

One of ancient Egypt's great cities was el-Amarna, but only for 15 years. Its Egyptian name was Akhetaten ("The Horizon of the Sun Disc"). When the pharaoh Akhenaten decided to build a new capital he chose a site that had never been inhabited before. Work began in about 1349 BC and the city spread rapidly to cover an area of about 2 sq. mi.

Brilliant palaces, temples and tombs
The city of el-Amarna became the chief royal residence and the center of government. There were at least five palaces and many official buildings. In the mud-brick palaces walls, floors and ceilings were painted or tiled in brilliant colors. One room in the North

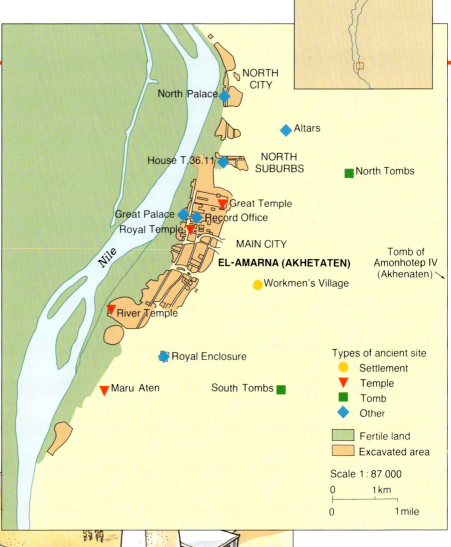

Types of ancient site
- 🟡 Settlement
- 🔻 Temple
- 🟩 Tomb
- 🔷 Other

🟩 Fertile land
🟧 Excavated area

Scale 1 : 87 000
0 — 1km
0 — 1mile

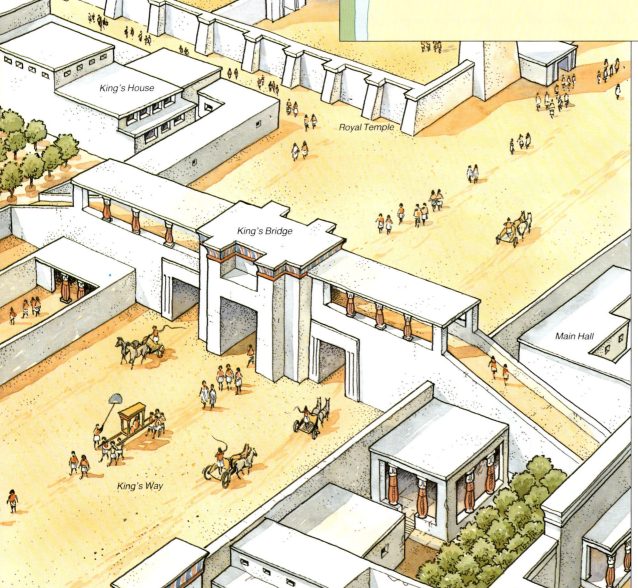

△ Plan of the areas of el-Amarna excavated so far. The temples and altars marked were all dedicated to the Sun Disc (Aten). The purpose of some buildings, such as the Maru-Aten, is uncertain. The workmen's village was lived in for some time after the main city was abandoned.

◁ This picture shows what part of the central city would have looked like c. 1340 BC. The "King's Way" was 130ft wide. At this point it passes under the "King's Bridge" which linked the "Great Palace" to Akhenaten's private apartments (the "King's House"). "The Great Palace" had a series of stone courts and halls used on state occasions. The "Royal Temple," built for the Aten, was the second largest in the city.

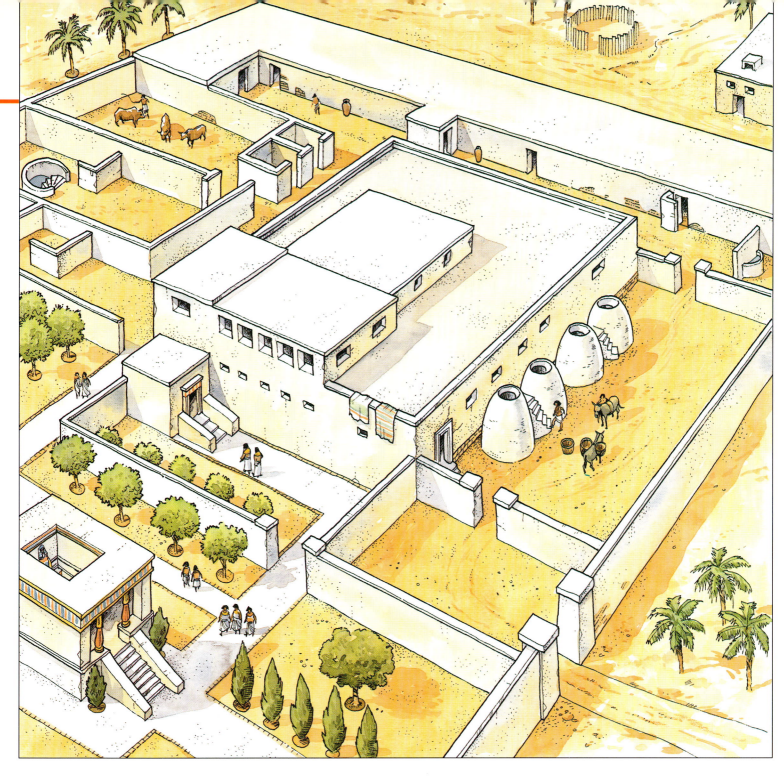

Palace had a marvelous painting of birds in a papyrus thicket covering three walls. Akhenaten's private apartments were decorated with charming pictures of Queen Nefertiti and the little princesses. Great officials such as the vizier also had finely decorated homes at el-Amarna.

The only deities worshiped at el-Amarna were the Aten (the Sun Disc) and Akhenaten himself. A new type of temple was built for the Aten. These temples had huge courtyards with hundreds of altars open to the sun.

Tombs were cut in the desert hills for the royal family and favored courtiers. Most

were never used but their reliefs give the official view of life in el-Amarna. In many scenes the rays of the Sun Disc end in hands holding out the symbol of life to Akhenaten.

The deserted city

Akhenaten's new ideas were not popular. He was called "The Great Criminal" after his death. In Tutankhamon's reign the city was deserted and never lived in again. Everything of value was taken away. Portraits of the disgraced royal family, including the famous head of Nefertiti (see page 18), were left behind in a sculptor's workshop.

△ The villa of a high official at el-Amarna. This reconstruction is based on the plan of a house known as T.36.11 (see plan). Such villas were like miniature farms. Fruit and vegetables were grown in the gardens. There were beehive-shaped grain bins (center right), a cattle yard and stalls and stables for chariot horses. Each villa had a shrine for worship of the Aten and the royal family (bottom left).

MEMPHIS

Memphis was the first capital of all Egypt. For three thousand years it was one of the country's greatest cities but little of that greatness survives. Most of Memphis is now buried deep under Nile silt or modern settlements. Remains of a few of the major buildings of Memphis can be seen in the palm groves around the village of Mit Rahina.

The chief deity of Memphis was the creator god Ptah. Only a small part of the temple complex of Ptah has been excavated. It was one of the largest temples in Egypt. Many kings were crowned there, including Alexander the Great. Palaces belonging to 19th- and 26th-Dynasty kings have been found at Mit Rahina.

A sacred bull

The god Ptah was represented by a sacred bull known as the Apis Bull. An Apis Bull had to have a white triangle on a black forehead, a scarab shape under its tongue and 27 other special marks on its body. The bull was kept in great luxury and led in procession once a year at the festival of "The Running of the Apis Bull". When the bull died it was mummified and placed in a huge stone sarcophagus.

From the time of Ramesses II the bulls were buried in underground galleries at Saqqara, part of the necropolis for Memphis. Above the galleries developed a temple known as the Serapeum. From the 3rd century BC the chief god of this temple was Serapis, who was created from Greek and Egyptian deities.

Cows who had given birth to Apis Bulls, sacred dogs, cats and ibises were also buried at Saqqara. Paying for the mummification and burial of a temple animal was thought to please the gods. Archaeologists exploring one set of galleries found the mummified bodies of over two million sacred ibises.

The great necropolis

The necropolis for Memphis stretches for 18mi along the edge of the Western Desert from Dahshur to Abu Rawash. It is probably the largest cemetery in the world. Among the royal tombs are step pyramids and true pyramids. From the 4th Dynasty each pyramid had two attached temples.

The valley temple was built on the edge of the floodplain so that it could be reached by boat.

Statues were kept in this temple to serve as extra bodies for the dead king. From the valley temple the royal coffin was taken up an enclosed causeway to the mortuary temple. This was usually on the east side of the pyramid because the king hoped to be reborn like the sun rising in the east.

Priests made offerings to the king's spirit in the mortuary temple. Sometimes this cult would continue for hundreds of years after a king had died.

Small subsidiary pyramids were also part of a pyramid complex. By the Middle Kingdom these were used for the burial of royal ladies. In the Old Kingdom some may have been for the king's vital organs. The *mastaba* tombs of high officials and members of the royal family are grouped around the Old Kingdom pyramids.

◁ A bronze statuette of an Apis Bull. Many bronze figures of deities were given to temples by pious Egyptians in the Late and Greco-Roman Periods.

▽ Tomb types in the Memphis necropolis:
1 *Mastaba tomb*, 1st-6th Dynasties.
2 *Step pyramid*, 3rd Dynasty.
3 *Bent pyramid*, 4th Dynasty.
4 *True pyramid*, Old and Middle Kingdoms.

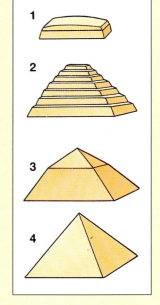

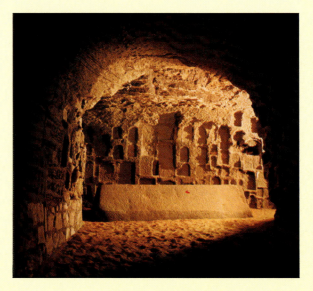

◁ One of the underground galleries of the Serapeum at Saqqara. The niches in the walls once held stelae left by pilgrims. About 1,200 of these stelae survive. The pilgrims came to take part in the burial rites of the Apis Bull and other sacred animals. Pilgrims that paid for the burial of a temple animal were often cheated by the embalmers, who bandaged up a few stray bones instead of a whole corpse.

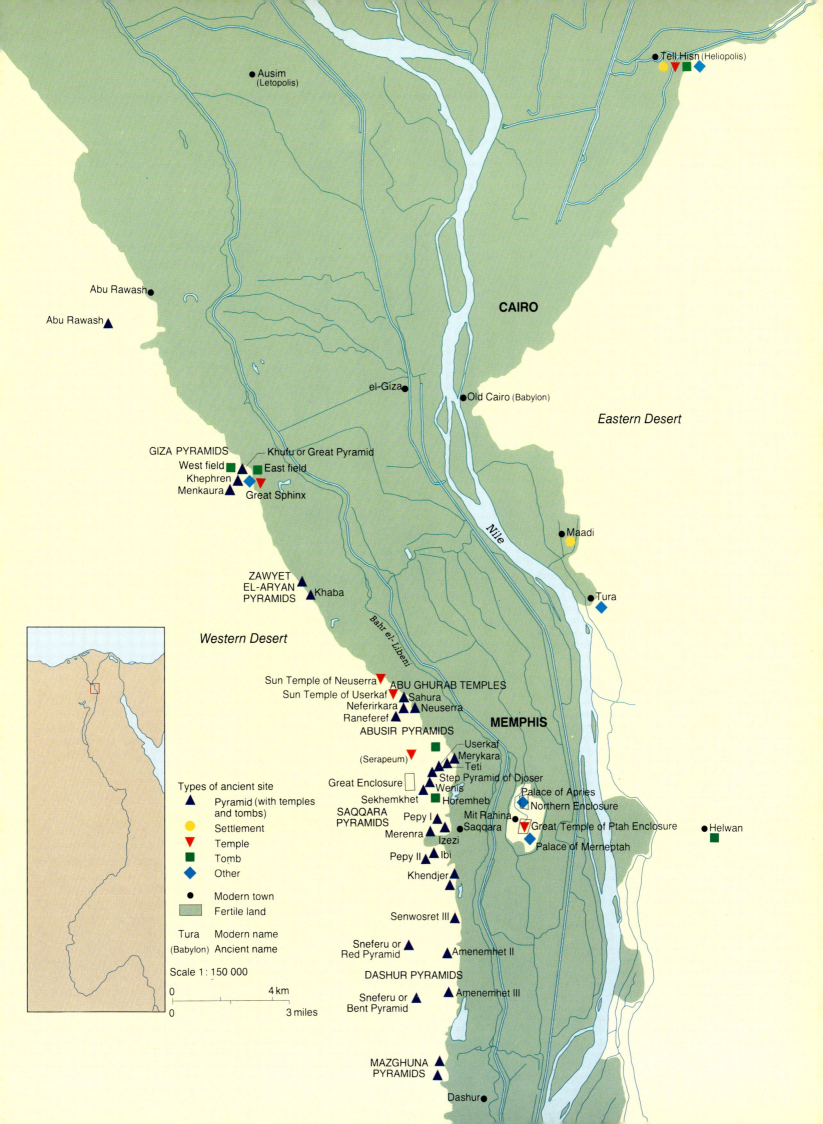

Ausim
(Letopolis)

CAIRO

Abu Rawash
Abu Rawash ▲

el-Giza •
Old Cairo (Babylon) •

Eastern Desert

Nile

Maadi •

GIZA PYRAMIDS
Khufu or Great Pyramid
West field ■ ▲ ■ East field
Khephren ▲ ◆ ▼
Menkaura ▲ Great Sphinx

Tura •
Tura ◆

ZAWYET
EL-ARYAN
PYRAMIDS ▲
▲ Khaba

Western Desert

Bahr el-Libeini

Sun Temple of Neuserra ▼ **ABU GHURAB TEMPLES**
Sun Temple of Userkaf ▼ ▲ Sahura
Neferirkara ▲ ▲ Neuserra
Raneferef ▲
ABUSIR PYRAMIDS

MEMPHIS

Userkaf
(Serapeum) ▼ ■ Merykara
▲ Teti
Great Enclosure ▯ ▲ Step Pyramid of Djoser
▲ Wenis
Sekhemkhet ▲ ■ Horemheb
**SAQQARA
PYRAMIDS**
Pepy I ▲ Mit Rahina ◆ Palace of Apries
Merenra ▲ • Saqqara ◆ Northern Enclosure
▲ Izezi ▼ Great Temple of Ptah Enclosure
Pepy II ▲ Ibi ◆ Palace of Merneptah
• Helwan
■
Khendjer ▲

Senwosret III ▲

Sneferu or ▲
Red Pyramid ▲ Amenemhet II

DASHUR PYRAMIDS
Sneferu or ▲ ▲ Amenemhet III
Bent Pyramid

**MAZGHUNA
PYRAMIDS** ▲
▲

Dashur •

Tell Hisn (Heliopolis) •
● ▼ ■ ◆

Types of ancient site
▲ Pyramid (with temples
and tombs)
● Settlement
▼ Temple
■ Tomb
◆ Other
● Modern town
Fertile land

Tura   Modern name
(Babylon) Ancient name

Scale 1 : 150 000

0   4 km
0   3 miles

Pyramids at Dahshur

Dahshur is the southernmost part of the necropolis of Memphis. Snofru, the first king of the 4th Dynasty, built two stone pyramids here. They are known as the Bent Pyramid and the Red Pyramid.

The Bent Pyramid

The Bent Pyramid was probably the first royal tomb to be designed as a true pyramid. When the pyramid was half-built the angle of the outer faces was suddenly reduced to give a gentler slope. At the same time a new method of laying the casing stones was introduced. These changes may have been made in order to prevent this pyramid collapsing like the one at Maidum. The Red Pyramid is a huge true pyramid built at the same angle as the upper part of the Bent Pyramid.

Royal treasures

Two 12th-Dynasty rulers, Senwosret III and Amenemhet III, built mud-brick pyramids at Dahshur. Two minor 13th-Dynasty kings were buried nearby. Six wooden boats were found in a pit near the pyramid of Senwosret III. The tombs of queens and princesses are grouped around the 12th-Dynasty pyramids. Wonderful jewelry has been recovered from six of these tombs. The royal ladies had crowns, necklaces, pendants, belts, bracelets and anklets. These were made in gold, lapis lazuli, turquoise, amethyst and cornelian.

△ Wooden statue of a king's *ka* (spirit) from a 13th-Dynasty tomb at Dahshur. The pair of arms on the head is the *ka* sign.

▽ The Bent Pyramid (left) and the Red Pyramid (far right) at Dahshur. In the foreground are two Old Kingdom royal tombs at Saqqara – showing how close together these two royal cemeteries are.

Cemetery at Saqqara

Saqqara was an important cemetery for over three thousand years. Kings were buried here at least as early as the 2nd Dynasty. The most famous monument is the Step Pyramid (see page 31) but there are 13 other pyramids at Saqqara. These range in date from the 3rd to the 13th Dynasties.

The writing on the walls

The pyramid of Wenis, the last king of the 5th Dynasty, is the earliest to be inscribed with the magic spells known as the Pyramid Texts. These spells were probably recited during the funeral. Their purpose was to help the king become a god in the afterlife.

The causeway of this pyramid is decorated with reliefs. There are scenes of boats bringing granite columns from Aswan to Saqqara and workers collecting honey. An inscription records repairs to the pyramid by a son of Ramesses II nearly 1,200 years after it was originally built.

Decorated tombs

From Early Dynastic times high officials were buried in *mastaba* tombs at Saqqara. The finest belong to important men of the 5th and

◁ This beautifully carved wooden panel from a Saqqara tomb is about 4,600 years old. It shows the "Chief of Dentists and Doctors," Hezyre.

▷ A tomb statue served as an extra body in case the mummy was destroyed. This statue of a Chief Priest from Saqqara has inlaid eyes. Plaster and paint would once have covered the wood. Successful men were often shown as middle-aged and fat. Fatness was a symbol of prosperity.

6th Dynasties. Their tombs have many small rooms decorated with painted reliefs. These show the tomb owner enjoying all the good things of life. Scenes in the family tomb of the Vizier Mereruka include a hippopotamus hunt, girls dancing, children playing leap-frog and dwarfs walking the household pets. Impressive statues have been found in some of the Old Kingdom tombs.

The next great age of tomb building at Saqqara was under the late 18th and early 19th Dynasties. High officials of this era had large stone tombs with pillared courts and chapels topped by miniature pyramids. The reliefs in the recently excavated tomb of General Horemheb are among the most beautiful ever carved in Egypt. In the Late Period a new "robber-proof" type of tomb appeared. The coffins were placed at the bottom of large deep shafts filled with a huge mass of sand.

△ A 6th-Dynasty tomb scene at Saqqara of cattle wading a canal. Fish and a hippopotamus are shown below the waterline.

▽ Egyptian guards with an Asiatic prisoner. A scene from the tomb built at Saqqara for Horemheb before he became king.

Buildings at Abusir & Abu Ghurab

The four 5th-Dynasty pyramids at Abusir were not very well constructed. The smooth casing blocks that once hid their rough core masonry have been stripped off to be reused in buildings or made into lime. This has happened to most other Egyptian pyramids.

The Pyramid of Sahura

The pyramid complex of King Sahura must have been impressive when it was intact. Most of the reliefs that once decorated its temples are lost. The few that survive show episodes from royal life. One fragment has the earliest scene of seagoing ships in Egyptian art. Another shows animals captured during a war with the Libyans. The inscription claims that this booty included 123,440 cattle and 243,688 sheep.

Sahura's successor Neferirkara planned a huge pyramid complex at Abusir but it was never completed. The causeway was taken over by the next king, Neuserra, for his pyramid complex. The fourth Abusir pyramid was built by King Raneferef. The largest of the *mastaba* tombs around these pyramids belonged to the vizier Ptahshepses. Graffiti of c.1229 BC show that this tomb was a tourist attraction in the New Kingdom.

Sun temples

Half-way between Abusir and Abu Ghurab, King Userkaf, founder of the 5th Dynasty, built a great temple to the sun god Ra. This structure has a causeway and valley temple as if it was a pyramid complex.

At Abu Ghurab a much better preserved Sun Temple dates to the reign of Neuserra. Its central feature was an open court with an altar and a giant obelisk built of limestone blocks. The obelisk was a copy of the sacred *benben* stone in the temple of Ra at Heliopolis. This stone was a symbol of the first mound of land and of the rays of the sun. The temple has a huge brick-built model of the boat of the sun god. "The Room of the Seasons" is also here. Painted reliefs show giant figures – the spirits of inundation, spring and harvest.

△ Part of the harvest season relief from the "Room of the Seasons" at Abu Ghurab. In the middle row an oryx is giving birth. At the bottom left are two hunting dogs.

▽ An alabaster (calcite) altar in the open court of the sun temple built by King Neuserra at Abu Ghurab. It is 20ft across. Three of the Abusir pyramids can be seen in the distance.

Pyramids at Giza

◁ Part of the valley temple of King Khephren's pyramid complex at Giza. It is built in limestone, alabaster and polished red granite.

▽ Riders on camels show the massive scale of the Great Pyramid at Giza. A few of the original smooth casing blocks can be seen at the bottom of the pyramid. The Giza pyramids are the only one of the Seven Wonders of the ancient world that survives.

The plateau of Giza is on the edge of modern Cairo. The area was used for burials at least as early as the 2nd Dynasty. The biggest of all Egyptian royal tombs were built here in the 4th Dynasty.

The Great Pyramid

The pyramid of Khufu (Cheops) at Giza is now known as the Great Pyramid. Its ancient name was "The Pyramid which is the place of Sunrise and Sunset." The original height was 482ft and it covers an area of 2,800 sq.yds. Nearly 4,500 years after it was built, the Great Pyramid is still one of the largest man-made structures in the world. There are five boat pits near this pyramid (see page 52).

Khufu's valley and mortuary temples have not survived. There are three subsidiary pyramids and many stone *mastaba* tombs.

The tomb of Khufu's mother, Queen Hetepheres, lies beside the causeway of the Great Pyramid. The canopic chest holding the queen's vital organs were found in this intact tomb but the sarcophagus was empty. Possibly Hetepheres' original tomb had been robbed and her body destroyed. Among the queen's treasure were 28 silver anklets decorated with butterflies. In the Old Kingdom silver was more valuable than gold.

The second and third pyramids

King Khephren built his pyramid beside that of his father Khufu. His pyramid (original height 473ft) is only slightly smaller than the Great Pyramid. The third Giza pyramid belongs to King Menkaura. It is much smaller and less impressive than the other two. Beautiful royal statues have been found in the valley temples of Khephren and Menkaura.

Near the valley temple of Khephren an outcrop of limestone was carved into a sphinx 240ft long. The Great Sphinx has the body of a lion and the head of a king – probably Khephren. In the New Kingdom the Great Sphinx was worshiped as a form of the sun god. A temple was built close to the Great Sphinx and many pilgrims left offerings.

PYRAMID CONSTRUCTION

Building the Old Kingdom pyramids was a gigantic task. The Great Pyramid at Giza contains about 6.25 million long tons of stone. The individual blocks weigh between 2 and 15 tons. To complete this pyramid during Khufu's reign, the blocks must have been produced at the rate of one every two minutes each day for 23 years. The stonemasons who quarried, shaped and smoothed the blocks formed a highly skilled permanent workforce.

Many of the blocks were quarried close to the pyramid site. Granite from Aswan and fine limestone from Tura were brought by barge to

▽ Building a pyramid. On this half-finished pyramid the central core and the stepped buttress walls can still be seen. Gangs of men are hauling limestone blocks up the building ramp. Water is poured on to the ropes and sledges to reduce friction (left). To the right, stonemasons are checking blocks for flatness and two architects are discussing their plan of the pyramid.

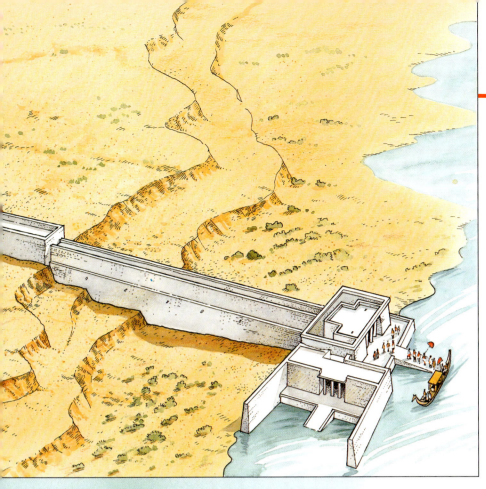

the edge of the desert. The blocks were then lashed on to sledges. They were dragged over wooden rollers, which had to be kept damp to prevent friction. Mud-brick ramps were probably used to get the stones up to where they were needed.

Inside each Old Kingdom pyramid is a series of stepped buttress walls around a central core. Packing blocks were used to fill in the steps. Then the casing stones were added. These were fitted closely to form the smooth outer walls. The casing stones were mainly of pale Tura limestone so the pyramids would originally

◁ A reconstruction of Sahura's pyramid complex at Abusir. A causeway joins the riverside valley temple to the courtyard of the mortuary temple. There is one subsidiary pyramid.

▽ Sahura's pyramid in a cutaway view. A passage runs from a hidden entrance on the north face to the burial chamber. Some blocks in the roof of this chamber are 36ft long.

have looked white. The capstone at the very top of a pyramid was covered in gold.

Empty burial chambers
The king's burial chamber was usually under the center of the pyramid. In the Great Pyramid the granite burial chamber is reached by a steeply ascending corridor known as the Grand Gallery. After Khufu's funeral huge granite blocks were slid down to seal off the burial chamber. These impressive precautions failed to stop the tomb robbers. No bodies or grave goods have been found in any of the Old Kingdom pyramids.

LOWER EGYPT — THE DELTA

Most of the ancient cities of the Delta were built on high ground beside branches of the Nile. The moist climate of the marshy Delta is not good for preserving ancient remains. Many archaeological sites have been lost because the course of river branches and the shape of the coastline have changed.

In more recent times other ancient buildings have been destroyed by people wanting stone for building work or mud-bricks to make into fertilizer. As a result we know much less about Lower Egypt than we do about Upper Egypt.

Unrobbed tombs

Old Kingdom remains are quite rare in the Delta and most of the Middle Kingdom sites are not well preserved. The Delta gained in importance from the 19th Dynasty onwards. In the late New Kingdom and for much of the Third Intermediate Period Egypt was ruled from the Delta. Kings and queens of the 21st and 22nd Dynasties were buried inside temple enclosures in Delta cities. Royal tombs of this kind have been found at Tanis, Tell Atrib and Tell el-Muqdam. They include some of the very few unrobbed royal burials to survive.

The Delta once had many temples as great as the ones that still stand in southern Egypt. The famous temple of the war goddess Neith at Sais has disappeared. The Late Period temple of Isis at Behbeit el-Hagar is unique in being built entirely in granite. This temple has now completely collapsed.

Alexandria

The Ptolemies built Egyptian-style temples all over the Delta but their capital, Alexandria, was a Greek city. It belonged to the Mediterranean world. Greeks and Egyptians lived in separate areas of the city. Alexandria's most famous building was a great lighthouse known as the Pharos. This was another of the Seven Wonders of the ancient world.

Some parts of ancient Alexandria have been claimed by the sea. Others are buried under the modern city. Underground tombs survive by the site of the temple of the Greco-Egyptian god Serapis. These tombs are decorated with scenes from Egyptian religion painted in Greek style. They show that the Greeks did borrow some ideas from their Egyptian subjects.

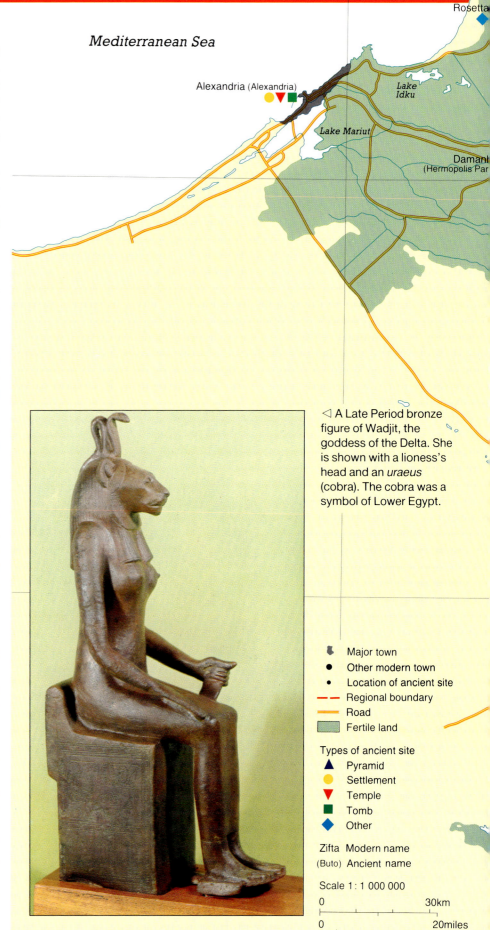

Mediterranean Sea

Rosetta

Alexandria (Alexandria)

Lake Idku

Lake Mariut

Damanl
(Hermopolis Par

◁ A Late Period bronze figure of Wadjit, the goddess of the Delta. She is shown with a lioness's head and an *uraeus* (cobra). The cobra was a symbol of Lower Egypt.

Major town
● Other modern town
· Location of ancient site
– – Regional boundary
— Road
Fertile land

Types of ancient site
▲ Pyramid
● Settlement
▼ Temple
■ Tomb
◆ Other

Zifta Modern name
(Buto) Ancient name

Scale 1 : 1 000 000
0   30km
0   20miles

Town at Bubastis

Bubastis was an important town from the Old Kingdom onwards. It was the chief cult center of the feline goddess Bastet. The main temple of Bastet was rebuilt many times. The 22nd Dynasty kings, who came from Bubastis, put up magnificent buildings for Bastet.

The annual festival of the goddess was one of the most popular in Egypt. People came from all over the country to sing, dance and feast in honor of Bastet. One Greek writer commented that *"More wine is drunk at this festival than in the whole of the rest of the year"* (Herodotus, *History II*).

From the Third Intermediate Period sacred cats were bred in the temple. A special cat cemetery lies to the north of the town. During the 19th century thousands of cat mummies from Bubastis were shipped to Europe to be ground up and used as fertilizer.

▽ Bronze statuette of a sacred cat from Bubastis. The cat wears a necklace and its ears are pierced for earrings. Probably dating to the Late Period.

Fort at Tell el-Yahudiya

Tell el-Yahudiya is famous for a mysterious earthwork known as the "Hyksos Camp." This rectangular enclosure, 567 × 539 yd, has huge defensive walls. It is unlike any other building in Egypt but it does resemble forts excavated in Palestine.

Some archaeologists think that it was a fortress built by the Hyksos. These were the foreign kings who seized power in the Delta in the Second Intermediate Period (see page 35). Pottery of Palestinian types has been found at Tell el-Yahudiya. It is thought by other archaeologists that the "Hyksos Camp" is a New Kingdom religious building.

Festival palaces
Several temples were built in or beside the enclosure during the late New Kingdom. Ramesses II set up the usual colossal statues of himself outside his temple. A temple built by Ramesses III had a palace attached. Such palaces were probably used by kings when they visited a temple to celebrate a religious festival. Some beautiful glazed tiles survive from this site. They show how dazzlingly colorful New Kingdom royal palaces must have been.

By this period the great city of Heliopolis had expanded up to the edge of Tell el-Yahudiya. Heliopolis was the chief cult center of the sun god Ra. Its main Sun Temple housed the sacred *benben* stone (see page 84). The High Priest of Heliopolis was usually one of the most important and influential men in ancient Egypt. Almost all of Heliopolis is lost beneath the northern suburbs of Cairo.

▽ Glazed faience tiles of lotus flowers, daisies and bunches of grapes. This row of tiles once decorated the wall of a palace of Ramesses III at Tell el-Yahudiya.

Treasures of Tanis

The ruins at Tanis are the most impressive in the whole of the Delta. Tanis was the capital of Egypt for much of the Third Intermediate Period. Inside a double mud-brick enclosure wall lies a great temple of Amon founded by King Psusennes I. This temple was added to by several Third Intermediate Period kings.

Stone blocks, columns, obelisks and statues of much earlier dates have been found at Tanis. All of these come from older buildings at other sites. They were brought to Tanis to give instant splendor to the new capital.

A golden discovery

In 1939 a French archaeologist named Pierre Montet found underground tombs near the southwest corner of the temple. Six Third Intermediate Period kings had been buried there. Some of the burials were intact. Spectacular gold and silver jewelry and vessels were recovered. King Psusennes I had a silver coffin and a golden mummy mask.

▽ A granite sphinx with the face of a 12th-Dynasty king. Later kings put their names on the statue. It was moved to Tanis in the Third Intermediate Period. Sphinxes were symbols of royal power and a form of the sun god.

City at Qantir

The Qantir area was twice of great importance in Egyptian history. In the Second Intermediate Period it was the site of Avaris, the capital of the Hyksos kings. Avaris was probably in the south part of the Qantir district, close to modern Tell el-Daba. This Hyksos city was taken and perhaps destroyed by the Theban king Ahmose in about 1540 BC.

The Ramessid family came from this area of the Delta. Ramesses II built a new city called Pi-Ramesses close to modern Qantir. It was one of the largest and most splendid cities in Egypt – the palace area alone covered nearly 22 acres (nine soccer pitches). Almost nothing is left. Many of the main buildings were later dismantled to provide stone and statues for Tanis. It was probably forced labor on the building of Pi-Ramesses that led to the Exodus of the Jews from Egypt.

▽ This bronze bust of a king probably comes from the Qantir area and may have been part of a statue.

91

GLOSSARY

Book of the Dead Spells written on papyrus and placed in tombs from the New Kingdom to the Greco-Roman Period. No single copy contains all 200 spells.

Canopic jars Set of four jars to hold the vital organs removed from a mummy. The organs were the liver, lungs, stomach and intestines.

Cartouche A sign representing an oval knot of rope. From the 4th Dynasty the king's two most important names were written inside cartouches. Cartouches were written on the King's documents and made into reliefs on the King's buildings and statues as a kind of seal.

Cataracts Stretches of dangerous rapids in the Nile. There were six cataracts between Aswan and Khartum in Sudan.

Colonnade A double row of columns roofed to form a passage or a single row of columns joined by a roof to a wall.

Cuneiform The Mesopotamian script, written on clay tablets with wedge-shaped strokes. Tablets with cuneiform texts were found at el-Amarna.

Deity A god or goddess. Many Egyptian deities can have human, semi-human and animal shapes.

Demotic An Egyptian script for everyday use, developed in the 7th century BC. It is one of the three scripts on the Rosetta Stone.

Dynasty A series of rulers, usually related to each other by blood or marriage. The order of the dynasties is known from the 3rd Century BC historian Manetho and from ancient Egyptian lists of kings.

Faience Egyptian faience (glazed pottery) was made by baking quartz sand with other mineral ingredients. The most common colors are green and blue.

Figurine A small statue of a god or goddess, a person or an animal. Figurines could be made of stone, wood, metal, faience or pottery.

Findspot Place where an ancient Egyptian remain or relic was found by archaeologists.

Hieratic An Egyptian script used on *papyrus* and *ostraca*. It was developed from the *hieroglyphic* script.

Hieroglyph A sign in the oldest Egyptian script. Most hieroglyphic signs are pictures of people, animals, plants or things. The word is Greek and means "sacred carving."

Inundation The annual flooding of the Nile between July and October. A "good Nile" was a flood that covered all the agricultural land, leaving behind a fertile layer of mud. If the flood was too high, it swept away houses. If the flood was too low, it would not cover all the fields. These were "bad Niles."

Ka The spirit or "double" of a living person. After death the *ka* needed offerings to survive. A dead person also had a *ba* (soul), shown as a human-headed bird.

Mastaba A type of Early Dynastic and Old Kingdom tomb with a flat-roofed rectangular superstructure. The name comes from the Arabic word for a bench.

Mummification The artificial preservation of bodies. Drying out the body was usually the most important part of the process.

Natron A natural mixture of carbonate, bicarbonate, chloride and sodium sulfate. It was used in *mummification* and was an ingredient of *faience*.

Necropolis A Greek term meaning "city of the dead." It is used for large and important burial areas. These were mainly on the edge of the desert.

Nome Greek word for an administrative province of Egypt. The governor of a nome was a *nomarch*.

Obelisk A tapering stone shaft with a tip shaped like a pyramid. A symbol of the Sun's rays. Pairs of obelisks were often set up outside temples.

Oracle A shrine where a god or goddess (deity) answered questions from worshipers or a sign given by a deity in answer to a question.

Ostracon A flake of limestone or a broken piece of pottery used for writing or drawing on. Most texts on ostraca are in *hieratic* or *demotic*.

Papyrus A marsh plant (*Cyperus papyrus*) and a type of paper made from it. Also a scroll made from sheets of papyrus gummed together.

Pharaoh A title for the king of Egypt from the late 18th Dynasty onwards. It means "The Great House" – the Palace.

Pylon The grand entrance to a temple, consisting of towers flanking a doorway.

Pyramid Tomb in the shape of a geometric pyramid. This shape may have symbolized a stairway to heaven, the Sun's rays or the first mound of land.

Relief A scene carved in stone or wood.

Sacred bark A special boat used by a statue of a deity on river journeys. Statues were often carried in model boats known as *bark shrines*.

Sarcophagus Used in this book to mean the stone chest that a coffin was placed inside. A sarcophagus was rectangular or anthropoid (human body-shaped).

Scarab A carving in the form of a scarab (dung-) beetle. It represented Khepri, god of the rising Sun. This "Sun beetle" was a very popular amulet shape. Scarabs were often inscribed with royal names.

Scribe A person trained to read and write. Most scribes worked for the government.

Shabti (or **Ushabti**) Small figurines, usually in the shape of a mummy, placed in burials. Their magical purpose was to carry out any work the dead person might be told to do in the afterlife.

Sphinx An Egyptian sphinx had the body of a lion and the head of a king or queen. It was a symbol of royal power and a form of the Sun God.

Stela A slab of stone or wood, usually with carved and painted texts and scenes. Stelae were set up in the outer areas of tombs and in temples somewhat like grave stones or commemorative plaques.

Uraeus A symbol of kingship in the shape of a rearing cobra,

Vizier The highest official in the Egyptian government. There were sometimes two viziers, one based at Memphis, the other at Thebes.

FURTHER READING

Picture Books
G.Hart *Ancient Egypt* (Octopus) 1988.
G.Harris *Gods and Pharaohs from Egyptian Mythology* (Schocken Books) 1982.
A.Langly *Cleopatra and the Egyptians* (Franklin Watts) 1986.
D.Macaulay *Pyramid* (Houghton Mifflin) 1989.
A.Millard *Pyramids* (Watts) 1989.
L.Manniche *The Lion and the Mouse: an Ancient Egyptian story* (British Museum Publications) 1984.
R.J.Unstead *Egypt and Mesopotamia* (A.& C.Black) 1977.

Reference books for adults
C.Aldred *Akhenaten, King of Egypt* (Thames & Hudson) 1988.
C.Andrews *Mummies* (British Museum Publications) 1984.
J.Baines & J.Malek *Atlas of Ancient Egypt* (Facts On File) 1988.
C.Desroches Noblecourt *Tutankhamen* (Michael Joseph) 1969
K.A.Kitchen *Pharaoh Triumphant: The Life and Times of Ramesses II* (Aries & Phillips) 1985.
A.Lurker *The Gods and Symbols of Ancient Egypt* (Thames & Hudson)1984.
G.Robins *Egyptian Paintings and Relief* (Shire) 1986.
A.J.Spencer *Death in Ancient Egypt* (Penguin) 1983.
A.Thomas *Egyptian Gods and Myths* (Shire) 1986.
P.Watson *Pyramids and Mastaba Tombs* (Shire) 1987.

GAZETTEER

The gazetteer lists places and features, such as islands or rivers, found on the maps. Each has a separate entry including a page and grid reference number. For example:

Abydos 59 B2

Sometimes a modern place also has an ancient name form. This name is added to the entry before the reference number. For example:

Aniba (Miam) 55 A2

All features are shown in italic type. For example:

Atbara, r. 11 D3

A letter after the feature describes the kind of feature:

d. district; *i.* island; *o.* oasis;
r. river

Abahuda 55 A2
Abnub 75 B1
Abu Kebir 89 C2
Abu Simbel 55 A2
Abydos 59 B2
Addis Ababa 11 D2
Aden 11 E2
Akhmim (Panopolis) 71 B2
Aksha 54 A2
Albert Nile, r. 11 C1
Alexandria (Alexandria) 11 C4, 88 A3
Allaqi, Wadi 55 C2
Amada 55 B2
Amman 11 D4
Aniba (Miam) 55 A2
Armant (Hermonthis) 59 B3
Aswan (Elephantine) 11 D4, 55 B4, 59 B2
Aswan Dam 59 B2
Aswan High Dam 55 B3, 59 B1
Asyut 11 C4, 75 B1
Asyut (Lykopolis) 71 B3, 75 B1
Atbara, r. 11 D3
Atfih (Aphroditopolis) 75 B3
Ausim (Letopolis) 89 C2

Baghdad 11 E5
Bahariya, o. 11 C4
Bahr Yusuf, r. 75 A2
Behbeit el-Hagar 89 C3
Beirut 11 D5
Beit el-Wali 55 B3
Benha 89 C2
Beni Hasan 75 A1
Beni Mazar 75 A2
Beni Suef 89 C1, 75 B3
Biga 59 B2
Bilbeis 89 C2
Birket Qarun (Lake Moeris) 75 A3, 89 B1
Blue Nile, r 11 D2
Buhen 54 A1
Burullus, Lake 89 B3

Cairo 11 C4, 89 C2
Catherine, Mount 11 D4

Chad 10 B3
Crete, i. 11 C5

Dabod 55 B3
Dairut 70 A3, 75 A1
Dakhla, o. 11 C4
Damanhur (Hermopolis Parva) 88 B3
Damascus 11 D5
Damietta 89 C3
Damietta Branch, r. 89 C2
Dashur 89 C1
Deir el-Gabrawi 75 B1
Deir el-Bersha 75 A1
Dendara (Iunet) 71 C2
Dendur (Tutzis) 55 B3
Dibeira East 54 A2
Dibeira West 54 A2
Dunqul, o. 11 C3

Eastern Desert 11 C4, 59 C4, 71 C2
Edfu (Apollinopolis Magna) 59 B2
Egypt 11 C4, 55 A2
el-Amarna (Akhetaten) 71 A3, 75 A1
el-Ashmunein (Hermopolis) 75 A1
el-Badari 71 B2
el-Bahnasa (Oxyrhynchus) 75 A2
el-Baqliya (Hermopolis Parva) 89 C2
el-Derr 55 B2
el-Fashn 75 A2
el-Hella (Contra-Lato) 59 B3
el-Hiba (Ankyronon Polis) 75 A2
el-Kab (Nekheb) 59 B3
el-Kharga, o. 11 C4
el-Khatana 89 C2
el-Kula 59 B3
el-Lahun 75 B3
el-Lessiya 55 B2
el-Lisht (Itjtawy) 75 B3, 89 C1
el-Mahalla el Kubra 89 C2
el-Mansura 89 C3
el-Maragha 71 B2
el-Matariya 89 D3
el-Minya (Menat-Khufu) 75 A2
el-Moalla 59 B3
el-Qasr wa'l Saiyad (Khenoboskion) 71 C2
el-Qusiya (Cusae) 75 A1
el-Rizeiqat 59 B3
el-Sheikh Said 75 A1
el-Simbellawein 89 C2
el-Wasta 75 B3, 89 C1
Esna (Latopolis) 59 B3, 71 C1
Ethiopia 11 D2
Euphrates, r. 11 E5

Faiyum, d. 11 C4, 75 A3, 89 B1
Farafra, o. 11 C4
Faras 54 A2

Gebel el-Silsila 59 B2
Gebelein (Per-Hathor) 59 B3, 71 C1
Gerf Hussein 55 B3
Girga (Thinis) 71 B2
Great Bitter Lake 89 D2

Hawara 75 A3
Helwan 89 C1
Hiw (Diospolis Parva) 59 B3, 71 C1

Idku, Lake 88 B3
Ihnasya el-Medina (Herakleopolis) 75 A3

Iraq 11 E5
Ismailia 89 D2
Ismailia Canal 89 C2
Israel 11 D5

Jerusalem 11 D4
Jordan 11 D4

Kafr el-Sheikh 89 B3
Khartoum 11 D2
Kom Abu Billo (Terenuthis) 89 B2
Kom el-Ahmar (Hierakonpolis) 59 B3
Kom el-Hisn 89 B2
Kom Medinet Ghurab 75 A3
Kom Mer 59 B3
Kom Ombo (Ombos) 59 B2
Kor 54 A1
Kurkur, o. 11 D3
Kuwait 11 E4

Lebanon 11 D5
Libya 10 B4
Libyan Desert 11 B4
Little Bitter Lake 89 D2
Lower Egypt, d. 89 B2
Lower Nubia, d. 55 A2
Luxor (Thebes) 59 B3, 71 C1

Maidum 75 B3
Mallawi 70 A3, 75 A1
Manfalut 71 A3, 75 A1
Manzala, Lake 89 C3
Mariut, Lake 88 A3
Medinet el-Faiyum (Krokodilopolis) 75 A3, 89 B1
Meir (Cusae) 75 A1
Memphis 89 C1
Merimda Beni Salama 89 B2
Middle Egypt, d. 71 B3, 75 A2, 89 B1
Minuf 89 B2
Mirgissa (Iqen) 54 A1
Mit Ghamr 89 C2
Mogadishu 11 E1

Nafud, o. 11 E4
Nag el-Madamud 71 C1
Naqada (Ombos/Nubt) 71 C1
Nasser, Lake 11 D3, 55 B3, 59 B1
Naukratis 89 B2
New el-Sebua 55 B2
New Kalabsha 55 B3
Nile, r. 11 D3, 59 B3, 71 B2, 75 B3
Northern Upper Egypt, d. 59 B4, 71 B2, 75 B1
Nubia, d. 55 B3, 59 B1
Nubian Desert 11 D3

Old el-Sebua 55 B2
Old Kalabsha (Talmis) 55 B3

Philae 55 B4, 59 B2
Port Said 89 D3

Qantir 89 C2
Qasr (Ibrim Primis) 55 B2
Qasr el-Sagha 75 A3
Qattara Depression 11 C4
Qaw el-Kebir (Antaeopolis) 71 B2
Qena (Kaine) 59 B4, 71 C2
Qift (Koptos) 59 B3, 71 C1
Qus (Apollinopolis Parva) 71 C1
Qustul 55 A2

Riyadh 11 E4
Rosetta 88 B3
Rosetta Branch, r. 89 B2
Sa el-Hagar (Sais) 89 B2
Saft el-Hinna (Per-Sopdu) 89 C2
Sahara Desert 10 A4
Samalut 75 A2
San'a 11 E2
San el-Hagar (Tanis) 89 C2
Saudi Arabia 11 E4
Seila 75 B3
Serra East 54 A2
Shibin el-Kom 89 B2
Shirbin 89 C3
Sidmant el-Gebel 75 A3
Sinai, Mount 11 D4
Siwa, o. 11 C4
Sohag 71 B2
Somalia 11 E2
Southern Upper Egypt, d. 55 B4, 59 B3, 71 C1
Southern Yemen 11 F3
Speos Artemidos 75 A1
Sudan 11 C2, 55 A1
Suez 89 D1
Suez Canal 11 D4, 89 D3
Syria 11 D5

Tafa (Taphis) 55 B3
Tahta 71 B2
Tanta 89 B2
Tell Abu Sefa (Sile) 89 D2
Tell Atrib (Athribis) 89 C2
Tell Basta (Bubastis) 89 C2
Tell el-Daba (Avaris/pi-Ramesses) 89 C2
Tell el-Farain (Buto) 89 B3
Tell el-Farama (Pelusium) 89 D3
Tell el-Maskuta (Pithom) 89 D2
Tell el-Muqdam (Leontopolis) 89 C2
Tell el-Timai (Thumis) 89 C2
Tell el-Ruba (Mendes) 89 C2
Tell el-Yahudiya (Leontopolis) 89 C2
Tell Hisn (Heliopolis) 89 C2
Tell Nabasha 89 C2
Tigris, r. 11 E5
Tihna (Akoris) 75 A2
Tima 71 B2
Timsah, Lake 89 D2
Tod 59 B3, 71 C1
Tripoli 10 A5
Tumilat, Wadi 89 C2
Tuna el-Gebel (Hermopolis) 75 A1
Tura 89 C1

Umm el-Qaab 71 B2
Upper Nubia, d. 55 A1

Valley of the Kings 59 B3, 71 C1

Wadi Halfa 11 C3, 54 A1
Wannina (Athribis) 71 B2
Western Desert 11 C4, 59 A3, 71 B1, 75 A2
White Nile, r. 11 D2

Yemen 11 E2

Zagazig 89 C2
Zaire 11 C1
Zawyet el-Amwat 75 A2
Zifta 89 C2

INDEX